PIES, PÂTÉS
AND TERRINES

D1512671

GLYNN

CONTENTS

Published exclusively for J Sainsbury plc
Stamford House Stamford Street
London SE1 9LL
by Martin Books
a division of Woodhead-Faulkner (Publishers) Limited
Fitzwilliam House 32 Trumpington Street
Cambridge CB2 1QY

First published 1988

Text, photographs and illustrations
© J Sainsbury plc 1988

Printed in Great Britain

THE AUTHOR

Glynn Christian is known nationally as a lively and innovative television cook and since 1980 has starred on 'Pebble Mill', 'Breakfast Time', 'Daytime Live' and 'The Food and Drink Programme'.

Delicatessen foods are one of his specialist subjects, and as well as the *Delicatessen Food Handbook* he has written several books on cheese.

He writes a monthly column for *Elle* and for *Wine* magazines and has just opened 'Kitchenclass', a new-style school of cookery demonstration in London, where each day a different famous writer, chef or restaurateur demonstrates and entertains with their latest ideas and recipes. His previous book for Sainsbury's was *British Cooking at its Best*.

INTRODUCTION

I don't think I would be where I am today if it were not for pâtés. During the late 1970s (when pâté suddenly appeared in every restaurant and most delicatessens), I built a kitchen underneath my own delicatessen on Portobello Road. Then I had to find something to make in it, and pâté seemed to be the thing. I began making a range with no additives or preservatives and was soon distributing them all over London – there was even an American pilot who flew them back to New York in his cockpit. Through the small fame the pâté brought I was asked to write my first book – on cheese – then more books on delicatessen food followed, and then regular radio and television work. Circumstances stopped the pâté-making after a few years, but my interest and pleasure in properly made pâtés has continued.

The particular culinary advantage of pâtés is their flexibility; they are perfect for a snack, the basis of a light meal, or the tantalising start to a bigger meal. And when you are entertaining they positively thrive on being made days in advance. For any sizeable buffet I always include a pâté or two, to which guests help themselves: an infallible way to get them to mix and to start talking. And pâtés are just as much at home on a scrubbed kitchen table as on a double damask cloth; they are able to adapt their intrinsic roughness or sophistication to the circumstances in a way which few of us manage half as well.

Modern preferences for a lower-fat diet, and the advent of refrigeration, mean that this technique of preserving meat using fat is less desirable and necessary. Yet with new types of fresh produce on the shelves, and with the advent of the food processor, the possibilities of these most versatile standbys have increased no end.

The confusion over what is a pâté and what is a terrine rages on, of course. Essentially I believe that a pâté is the product and the terrine is the dish in which it is baked. You may argue that 'terrine' is also the word for a cooked pâté that is turned out of its container, or one which is served from it; it will taste the same, which is more important. British 'potted' foods are virtually the same. I wouldn't be at all surprised if the word were based on pâté; so much of our food vocabulary derives from French words. The real British equivalent of French pâté-making is sausage-making.

When all is said and done, there is little mystery to making pies, pâtés and terrines. The essential techniques are very few, and once you have cooked a few which appeal to you it is easy to branch out and make your own. Simply by varying the texture you will achieve a different flavour and appearance. But be bold; the major faults of any unsuccessful pâté are usually but two: far too much onion, or far too little of the flavourings. But all that is explained in the next section. I know you'll enjoy using this book. Pies, pâtés and terrines are all food to be shared; and that is the best reason to cook anything.

THEORY AND TECHNIQUES

Ingredients

If you remember that pâtés and terrines are essentially methods of preserving meats, it should be no surprise that fat is an important constituent of traditional recipes. Fat both binds and seals the cooked pâté, protecting it from air; and of course it adds a great deal of flavour. It is possible to make almost fatless pâtés of a sort, using gelatine as in the recipe for No-bake Fish Terrine (page 34), for instance; they are modern and unusual, however, and rarely use meat as the main ingredient.

Some recipes use bread, eggs, or, believe it or not, a choux pastry mixture as a binder. They are all good, but each dilutes the flavour of the meat and herbs, and if there is not also a high fat content you will end up with something more akin to a low-quality sausage or a meat loaf, with which pâtés are too often confused. The best alternative binder is ground almonds; they add a richness to any mixture without radically interfering with the flavour (see the recipe for Almond-potted Partridge with White Grapes, page 43); but they are expensive. A proper pâté mixture needs little extra binding, unless you intend to remove it from its cooking container and slice it theatrically before a discerning audience. Personally, I don't trust pâtés served at home that slice too beautifully: they look as though they have been made by commercial means.

The fat for pâté mixtures may come from three main sources: from the meat itself; from added pork of some sort (including bacon); or from butter and cream or a low-fat alternative like fromage frais in the case of fish pâtés. The firm back fat of pork, which keeps its shape when minced and cooked, is used for texture and contrast of appearance; the softer fat of belly pork is more usually minced rather finely with the meat in the expectation that it will render and dissolve during cooking, thus binding and flavouring the pâté. If ready-minced pork is not available, buy belly of pork or shoulder and mince it yourself.

I can't understand the people who say bacon should not be used in pâté mixtures. I never make a meat pâté without using bacon, especially if it is to be stored. Bacon is cured with saltpetre, a phenomenally effective bactericide which keeps pickled meats fresh and safe when uncooked. Once cooked, saltpetre turns the flesh an attractive pink colour, and this is also what it does in a pâté mixture. Much better to look at altogether, and you need very little to get this effect. Generally, the bacon specified in these recipes is green or unsmoked bacon, but I often substitute smoked bacon; it goes marvellously with most of the meats and birds suited to potting and pâté-making. But it is a stronger flavour and you will need less additional salt, or none at all.

If you are using the less fatty flesh of venison or of a game bird, it will be necessary to add much more fat than if you are making one mainly of pork. Usually, a balance of fatty belly of pork and bacon is best; however, both have their distinct advantages. Belly of pork is sweet when cooked and includes a lot of fat, so it balances harsh flavours and absorbs and spreads the fragrances of fresh herbs, spices, onions, garlic and wine, once the pâté is cooked and matured. Fatty bacon does much the same thing, adding stronger flavour and extra salt, and thus should be used more moderately.

Meat, then, is ideally fatty, but it really must also be free of gristle and sinews if it is to be put raw into pâté mixtures. No matter how long the cooking time, gristle and sinew will never soften in a pâté mixture. If the meat is not fatty, lots of fat must be added; in this I disagree profoundly with the so-called classic French school of pâté-making, in which one makes, say, a partridge pâté, by quickly roasting the bird, cutting off the breast and other useful flesh and then baking it in layers, with the minced pork or bacon to incorporate fat . The partridge flesh is usually over-powered by the pork, whereas clearly the intention was that the partridge should perfume the pork. I don't think this is possible, unless you do it my way. That is first to cook the meat or bird in a liquid, so the flavour of the bones is also extracted and what fat there is renders into the liquid. The flesh is removed from the bones and the cooking liquid reduced to an essence. The meat and this essence are both combined with a pork and bacon base that they are then strong enough to dominate. Herbs and spices are added, and this way one or two small birds can successfully and identifiably flavour a large amount of pork base.

The most important additional flavourings to pâté are usually considered to be herbs. I have clearly indicated whether fresh or dried should be used. More important than this is the actual amount. A pinch of this or of that is quite useless in a pâté mixture. Herbs have two battles to fight if their flavour is to feature at all in the cooked product. First there must be enough of them to counteract both the blandness and the palate-coating effect of the fat content. And there must also be enough to stand up to the dissolution of their flavour by the long cooking times. Some herbs simply will not survive, or will do so in a rather bitter version of their original, fresh flavour – parsley for instance. I find spices work much better. Nutmeg is indispensable with pork-based mixtures, cloves are especially good if you have included orange zest and allspice is perhaps the best of all. If ever you have made a pâté rather more feeble in flavour than you had hoped, spices would certainly have saved it. I have also found that thyme is a far better friend to pork than sage; the combination of pork and thyme is found in old British recipes and thyme and nutmeg together become very special.

And now to another controversial subject: the use of onion. It is important that the amounts of onion stipulated in these recipes are kept to fairly closely. Too much onion in a pâté mixture upsets the liquid-to-fat ratio, preventing a good set. If you wish to keep the mixture for a while before cooking it, the acidity of excess onion is likely to sour or oxidise the pâté and the flavour will 'go off'. In a cooked pâté, an excess of onion will overpower any delicacy of flavour there is and encourage early and fast souring and moulding. Onion is, of course, an important and useful base for flavouring, but it must be used with discretion or you might as well stop here and simply spread onion on a slab of bread.

Wine and cognac are also commonly used, especially for marinating before cooking, but beware of using small amounts. Cognac or cheaper brandy will be dissipated easily unless added in substantial quantities, and if you really want a wine flavour it is actually best to concentrate the flavour by reducing it first.

Equipment

For traditional styles of pâté, the *mincer* is unquestionably the cook's best friend in handling the raw ingredients. Whether hand-operated or electric, mincers give an even-textured mixture. For fine pâtés, or to give a contrast of texture in a single pâté, you may have to mince some or all of the mixture twice, but always chill it between the operations; you do not want to overheat the mixture and affect the fat texture at this stage.

Today many people are likely to have a *food processor* and providing the blades are sharp they give a very good result. But don't fall into the trap of believing that food processors magically take all the trouble out of mincing and chopping, leaving you nothing to do. You must cut the meat into chunks, because long pieces wind themselves around the blade and spindle, especially if fatty. And you must work in small batches, alternating fatty and lean meats, or you will break down the texture unnecessarily through overheating due to the longer processing time. This also applies when you combine your fatty and lean meats afterwards.

If you are making a purée of cooked ingredients, of chicken livers or fish perhaps, a food processor works best with as little liquid as possible. If there is a lot of liquid, leave most of it to one side and add it after the mixture is approaching the texture you want.

A *liquidiser* works in exactly the opposite way. It will not mince or chop dry ingredients or make a purée of them, but a wet mixture is puréed faster and more successfully by a liquidiser than a food processor. I have indicated which I think is the more suitable throughout the book for each recipe, but you may have to adapt according to your equipment.

For both machines it really is worth working in small batches. You might get away with larger ones, but you run the risk of overheating, jamming or having to process everything twice, all of which would take up much more time altogether.

Containers

For pâtés and terrines, the most useful containers are loaf tins of cast iron. They give an even distribution of heat and a nice shape. In fact anything which is ovenproof can be used – glass and earthenware included – but those which taper slightly make it easier to remove the cooked pâté. Even well-used, straight-sided cake or bread tins can be successful. The only caveat when using something other than a loaf tin is that if the mixture is then flatter or thinner you will have to reduce the cooking time; if it is deeper and chunkier you will have to extend it.

If the mixture is light-coloured, metal containers may discolour it; in this case I line the tins with cling film if it is a roughish mixture or with blanched vine leaves if smooth. The latter is a terrific but easy way to make any pâté look better when turned out and the leaves add a delicious syrupy flavour, too.

It is thought traditional and proper to line pâtés and terrines with strips of bacon, and it can be jolly good on a few rugged mixtures; but generally this bacon coating also changes the balance of a carefully constructed flavour – it generally dominates in a game-bird pâté for instance. Use it very sparingly and only on the most robust mixtures, first stretching each slice with the back of a knife and, perhaps, also lightly blanching it to remove as much of the salt as you can.

Cooking

1

Most pâtés and terrines are better if cooked in a bain-marie, which is simply a French way of saying a water bath. This gives a more even distribution of temperature and stops burning and catching on the edges.

The best and safest way to arrange a bain-marie is to half-fill a roasting tin with hot water and to put this into the oven when you turn it on to preheat. By the time the pâté is ready to cook and the oven at the right temperature, the water will also be at the right temperature and you can put the pâté in the bain-marie, as in illustration 1. This is a simpler and safer way than pouring boiling water into the roasting tin.

To test if a pâté mixture is cooked, push a thin skewer or knitting needle into the centre and press lightly around the edges of the hole it leaves. If the liquid is clear the mixture is cooked; if it is cloudy or even slightly pink the pâté needs more cooking.

Once the pâté is cooked you might want to press it, which makes it firmer and easier to cut; it also squeezes out much of the fat and cooking liquids that I think should be retained in the end product. But if you do want a firm texture, lay some cling film over the pâté and then put weights on top. It is easier to use unopened bags of rice or pulses – which can be moulded to the shape you have made, as in illustration 2 – than boards and weights.

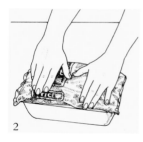

2

Storing

Most pâtés shouldn't be eaten for two days at least, giving them time for the flavours to mix and develop. This makes them perfect party and buffet food, as they can be made well in advance and then forgotten for a week or more. To do this, though, you must make certain that the pâté is well sealed against the air. Once it is cooked and set, turn it out from its container and scrub that clean. Then replace the pâté and seal the top and bottom with melted fat, butter or a mixture. You can flavour this for added interest, for example making an orange and nutmeg butter to seal a duck pâté. Sainsbury's Concentrated Butter is excellent for this. Wrap the pâté in foil tightly before storing it.

An uncut, high-fat pâté can generally be stored in the fridge for 2–3 weeks. Once cut, refrigerate the pâté as soon as possible and try to use it up in a few days. I have kept pies for a week before cutting them; it is best to finish them within a few days of their being cut. I don't think it's worth freezing pies or pâtés: freezing will break down the aspic in pies, and the high fat content of most pâtés means that freezing is not suitable.

Serving

All mixtures should be served chilled, so they slice better. And please, please don't pre-slice for guests. Even if you have added bacon and left the pâté long enough to develop a gorgeous rosy glow it will oxidise and turn a horrid grey-brown. And there is no need always to serve pâté with toast, which is a great bore to make for anything more than two people. Instead, scoop the pâté and arrange it on a bed of interesting and contrasted salad leaves. Sprinkle both pâté and salad with a decent dressing of very good oil and vinegar to add a sparkle and serve with knives and forks. For an even more startling departure, sprinkle the pâté and the salad with a little vodka, plain or flavoured.

Raised pies

A round cake tin with a removable base gives excellent results and is inexpensive. If you don't have one, a fully lined solid-based tin will do nicely. The fancy French moulds that clip together give professional results very easily but are expensive and only worth having if you make a lot of pies, unless you acquire one as a gift.

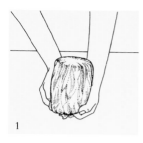

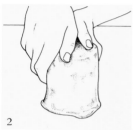

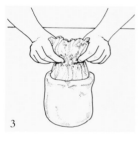

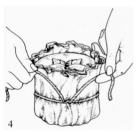

Of course, you can make raised pies without a secondary container at all, taking advantage of the qualities of hot-water pastry to bake the mixture in the solid pastry only. Once you have made the pastry, and whilst it is still warm, choose any dumpy, straight-sided container of the correct capacity. Cover it with cling film tightly (illustration 1), and then mould the pastry around it (on the outside, illustration 2). When the pastry is dry and firm, lift out the jar or container, using the cling film to help (illustration 3). Tie a triple-thick band of greaseproof paper around the pastry case to support it (illustration 4). Leave the paper in place for three-quarters of the cooking period; then remove it and glaze the sides with beaten egg so they brown nicely.

If you are using a tin in which to bake the pie, the usual rules and good sense apply. Ensure the pastry is evenly spread, and is not bunched up in the corners or around the edges of the base. Leave enough at the top to allow a firm seal with the lid, which should be wetted with water or egg yolk and pinched very firmly into place. Always make an air hole in the centre. It needs to be quite big so the filling dries slightly during cooking, and even if it gets blocked up can be enlarged when the time comes to pour in the aspic. If the aspic leaks out of holes in the pastry when you pour it in, let the pie cool and then plug the holes with butter and refrigerate until set hard. Then continue pouring in the aspic, which should be as cool as possible but not starting to set.

If you wish to make pastry leaves, flowers, initials and the like, you must make them large, for they will shrink during cooking. They should be glazed twice with beaten egg – once before going into the oven and again about halfway through cooking. The exception to this is when you want to decorate your pies with colour and pattern. This is simply done by painting the raw pastry with undiluted food colouring. Leave the colouring to dry and do not glaze until the last 20–30 minutes. If you are not artistic, simply painting lines on the diagonal, or writing 'Merry Christmas' in a bright colour, is startling enough to be worthwhile.

Serving portions

For a *first course* I estimate 25–40 g (1–1½ oz) per person, but I find that this varies according to the texture and richness of the pâté. A chunky pâté looks mean in small wedges, and as you pick up more at a time with your knife or fork, it is best to have closer to 75 g (3 oz) per person. A rich, creamy, mousse-like pâté is eaten in smaller amounts, but anything less than 25–40 g (1–1½ oz) will also look mean – unless it is meant to be a *bonne-bouche* atop a plate of intriguing salad leaves.

For *main courses*, with salad and the like, 75–125 g (3–4 oz) per person is about right, with the same provisos as above.

For *buffets*, there are appearances to consider. If you only put out what you expect people to eat it will look like village-fête catering, and everyone will be afeared of taking any at all in case others starve or they are considered greedy. At a drinks party, where the pâté is the most substantial thing on offer (and this is a terrific and easy way to entertain) 50 g (2 oz) per person of each of two different pâtés is a minimum, and more is better. When the pâtés are intended as the first course at a buffet or part of the choice of cold meats and poultry, you can reduce that to 40 g (1½ oz) of each of two pâtés. Interestingly, if you offer three pâtés instead of two your guests will still eat the same amount of each, provided there is genuine contrast between them. But always make more, for if it is a decent party you will be too tired to cook the next day and the leftovers will be just what you want.

PIES

HOT-WATER PASTRY FOR RAISED PIES

Preparation time: 10 minutes

375 g (12 oz) plain flour

1 teaspoon salt

150 ml (¼ pint) water

125 g (4 oz) lard, cut into small pieces

Hot-water pastry is used for traditional veal, ham and pork pies as it holds its shape better than an ordinary shortcrust. Unlike most other types of pastry, hot-water crust should be made at the last minute, should not be chilled, and in fact should be kept warm so it does not dry out. If uncooked, it does not keep well.

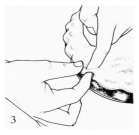

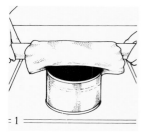

Sieve the flour with the salt; make a well in the centre. Heat the water with the lard until the lard has melted; pour this mixture into the flour. Mix to a soft dough and knead until smooth. Keep warm, covered, or it will dry out.

To line a tin with pastry, first cut off about a quarter of the dough for the lid and set it aside in a warm place, well wrapped. Press out the remaining dough to a suitable–size circle or square, depending on the size and shape of your tin; use your hands rather than a rolling pin to do this, for speed and to keep the dough warm.

Carefully fold the pastry back over a rolling pin and use the rolling pin to transfer it to the tin (illustration 1). Ease the pastry into the tin, pressing it well into the sides with your knuckles (illustration 2). Add the filling.

Use a rolling pin to roll the remaining dough into a smooth lid, using the tin as a guide for size, but making the lid about 1 cm (½ inch) bigger all round, to allow for shrinkage. Wet the edges of the pastry case, lift on the lid and squash the edges together firmly. Then deeply crimp the edges using the thumb and one finger of one hand and a finger or thumb of the other (illustration 3). (You can also use the handle of a spoon to make deep, decorative impressions.)

MY BASIC PORK PIE

Preparation time: 1 hour
+ 2 hours cooking + cooling

Makes about a 1.5 kg (3 lb) pie

875 g (1¾ lb) minced pork

50 g (2 oz) very finely chopped onion

150 ml (¼ pint) dry white wine, plus extra

2 tablespoons cognac

½ teaspoon dried sage or thyme

1 generous tablespoon Dijon mustard

1 small eating apple, peeled and grated coarsely

1 teaspoon salt

1 quantity of hot-water pastry (page 15)

beaten egg, to glaze

1 packet of aspic powder

black pepper

Oven temperatures:
Gas Mark 6/200°C/400°F
Gas Mark 4/180°C/350°F

Many a pork pie is simply minced pork with salt and pepper and little else: such blandness, though quintessentially British these days, is hardly worth reproducing at home. Here is something with a little more flavour to repay your effort and time.

Preheat the oven to the first setting. Mix the minced pork with the onion, wine, cognac, herbs, mustard, apple and seasoning. Line a 15 cm (6-inch), round, loose-based cake tin with three-quarters of the pastry (keep the remainder wrapped in cling film in a warm place). Pack the lined tin with the meat mixture; roll out the remaining pastry and fit the lid. Make a hole in the lid and pull back the edges. Decorate and glaze the pie with beaten egg, and then put it on a baking tray and bake for 30 minutes. Reduce the oven to the lower temperature and continue cooking for a further 1½ hours.

When the cooked pie has cooled, make up the aspic jelly with half the recommended liquid, using white wine rather than water for extra flavour. Pour it through the hole in the lid, slowly and in stages, until the pie will absorb no more. Once the aspic has set, wrap the pie and store it for a couple of days before cutting it.

VARIATION

If you choose to make this pie in a loaf tin you might consider putting a line of shelled hard-boiled eggs down the middle, as in the Veal, Ham and Egg Pie (page 20).

My Basic Pork Pie
Mustard, Veal, Rice and Egg Pie

MUSTARD, VEAL, RICE AND EGG PIE

Preparation time: 40 minutes
+ 1 hour cooking

Makes about a 1.25 kg (2½ lb) pie

375 g (12 oz) puff pastry

175 g (6 oz) long grain rice

2 eggs

3 tablespoons double cream

500 g (1 lb) minced veal

50 g (2 oz) butter, melted

25 g (1 oz) onion, chopped
finely

1 generous tablespoon Dijon
mustard with seeds

4 tablespoons chopped fresh
parsley, including stalks

4 hard-boiled eggs, shelled
and sliced

beaten egg, or milk, to glaze

salt and freshly ground black
pepper

Oven temperatures:
Gas Mark 7/220°C/425°F
Gas Mark 4/180°C/350°F

Baked flat like a large pasty, this attractive pie is wonderfully tasty without being aggressive. The creamy rice coating is the perfect foil for minced veal subtly flavoured with mustard; the mustard loses most of its bite during the baking but retains its fascinating finer flavours.

Preheat the oven to the first setting. Using approximately one-third of the pastry, roll out a 22 cm (9-inch) diameter circle. Put it on a wetted baking tray, prick it all over with a fork and bake it in the oven for 15 minutes. Remove it from the oven and allow to cool.

Cook the rice in twice its volume of water until just tender, by which time all the water should be absorbed. Stir the rice, raw eggs and cream together; season generously with salt and pepper. In a separate bowl, mix the veal, melted butter, onion, mustard and half of the chopped parsley. Season well.

Layer one-third of the rice mixture on the cooked pastry base; pile the meat on top and level it off to a uniform thickness. Cover with the sliced, hard-boiled eggs and sprinkle with the remaining parsley. Cover the top and sides of the meat evenly with the remaining rice mixture. Roll out the rest of the pastry to a circle comfortably big enough to cover the filling. Lift it on to the pie and tuck the edges under the base, without stretching. Dampen the pastry edges with water; seal and crimp them firmly, or lightly slash the edges to make a pattern without breaking through to the filling. Slash the top through to the filling in a couple of places and push the pastry back, to ensure the holes do not close up during cooking. Decorate the pie with pastry shapes if you like.

Brush the pastry with beaten egg, or milk, and bake in the oven for 10 minutes. Reduce the oven temperature to the second setting and bake for a further 50 minutes or until you are sure the pastry is properly cooked through. Serve warm or lightly chilled.

NO-TIME PORK AND STUFFING PIE

Preparation time: 20 minutes + 1¼ hours cooking

Makes about a 1 kg (2 lb) pie

500 g (1 lb) puff pastry

500 g (1 lb) minced pork

83 g (3 oz) packet of stuffing mix with Garlic and Herbs

150 ml (¼ pint) white wine

2 eggs

Oven temperatures:
Gas Mark 6/200°C/400°F
Gas Mark 4/180°C/350°F

It is a salient reminder, particularly to those who think cooking should be complicated or expensive to be appreciated, that this simple recipe, made in minutes, probably elicited the most favourable responses of any in this book. You can make it more robust with extra onion and seasoning if you like, and any stuffing mix except a sage and onion one can be used, with 1–2 chopped cloves of garlic.

Preheat the oven to the first setting. Roll out just under half the pastry to make a circle at least 25 cm (10 inches) in diameter; place it in the centre of a metal baking tray. Combine the pork, stuffing mix and wine. Separate the eggs and thoroughly beat 1 yolk and both whites into the pork mixture. Arrange in an even mound on the pastry base, leaving a generous border around the edge. Roll out the remaining pastry so that it will cover the pie comfortably, without stretching. Dampen the border and firmly seal the top to the bottom; then fold up the edges and crimp them deeply with your fingers or a fork. Make a couple of generous air holes in the top of the pie. Decorate it with any bits of leftover pastry if you so wish, but there is no need for there to be either excess pastry or decoration.

Whisk the remaining egg yolk lightly and then brush it over the pastry; bake the pie in the oven for 15 minutes. Reduce the oven to the second setting and continue cooking for a further hour, or until you are absolutely sure that the pastry is cooked right through, covering the pie with double greaseproof paper when the pastry is brown enough. Serve the pie warm, or leave it to cool; by this time the flavours will have developed further, of course.

VEAL, HAM AND EGG PIE

Preparation time: 20 minutes
+ 1¾ hours cooking + cooling

Makes about a 1.5 kg (3 lb) pie

1 quantity of hot-water pastry (page 15)
500 g (1 lb) minced veal
375 g (12 oz) ham, diced
1 teaspoon dried marjoram
1 tablespoon chopped fresh parsley
1 teaspoon finely grated lemon zest
2 tablespoons sherry or madeira, plus extra
½ teaspoon freshly grated nutmeg
½ teaspoon or so salt, according to saltiness of ham
3 or 4 hard-boiled eggs, shelled
seasoned flour
beaten egg, to glaze
1 packet of aspic powder

Oven temperatures:
Gas Mark 4/180°C/350°F
Gas Mark 3/160°C/325°F

Veal, Ham and Egg Pie

Once egg is included in a raised pie, it is usual to bake it in an oblong loaf tin rather than a round tin, so the egg will be evenly divided. You can make this without the eggs, naturally.

Preheat the oven to the first setting. Line with greaseproof paper the base of a 1.2-litre (2–pint) loaf tin and line the tin with three-quarters of the pastry. Keep the remainder wrapped in cling film in a warm place.

Mix the veal, ham, herbs, lemon zest and sherry or madeira together; season well with nutmeg and salt. Put half the mixture into the pie case. Toss the eggs in seasoned flour and arrange them on the meat. Cover with the rest of the meat mixture.

Roll out the reserved pastry as a lid and cover the pie. Seal the edges and crimp them deeply and decoratively. Cut several holes right through the top of the pastry and push them apart to ensure that they cannot close as the pastry swells during cooking. Bake for 30 minutes at the first setting; reduce the heat to the second setting and continue cooking for 30 minutes. Paint the top of the pie with the beaten egg glaze and return to the oven for another 45 minutes. Leave the pie to cool.

Once the pie is almost cool, make up the aspic using half the recommended liquid; use a goodly portion of the same sherry or madeira incorporated into the pie. Slowly pour it, in stages, through the top of the pie. Then let it set and leave the pie for a day or two before cutting into it.

Beef and Mushroom Pie

Pork, Veal, Apple
and Prune Pie

21

PORK, VEAL, APPLE AND PRUNE PIE

Preparation time: 20 minutes soaking
+ 40 minutes + 1¾ hours cooking + cooling

Makes about a 1 kg (2 lb) pie

50 g (2 oz) stoned prunes	
4 tablespoons dark rum	
1 quantity of hot-water pastry (page 15)	
375 g (12 oz) minced pork	
125 g (4 oz) unsmoked bacon, minced	
175 g (6 oz) minced veal	
125 g (4 oz) grated apple	
1 teaspoon ground cinnamon	
beaten egg, to glaze	
1 packet of aspic powder	
salt and pepper	

Oven temperatures:
Gas Mark 6/200°C/400°F
Gas Mark 3/160°C/325°F

Cumberland, now called Cumbria once again, was famous for a raised pie of pork and apple, and there are plenty of recipes for making it. This is a delicious variant which includes prunes; it makes a marvellous cold meal for weekends, especially over long holidays.

Preheat the oven to the first setting. Cut the prunes into quarters and pour half the rum over them; leave to soak for 20 minutes. Line a 15 cm (6-inch), round, loose-based cake tin with three-quarters of the pastry. Keep the remainder wrapped in cling film, in a warm place.

Mix together the minced meats, grated apple, cinnamon and seasoning. Press half the mixture into the lined tin, arrange the prunes with their soaking liquid evenly on top and cover with the remaining meat mixture.

Roll out the reserved pastry to form a lid and cover the pie. Crimp the edges deeply. Cut a hole in the lid and pull back the pastry so the hole will not close up during cooking. Stand the tin on a baking sheet and bake for 30 minutes. Glaze with the beaten egg. Reduce the heat to the lower setting and continue cooking for a further 1¼ hours, covering the top loosely with a sheet of foil if the pastry becomes too brown towards the end of cooking.

Once the pie is almost cool, make up the aspic powder with half the recommended amount of liquid and stir in the remaining rum. Pour it slowly into the pie (it may take some time and must be done in stages). Allow to set in the refrigerator.

BEEF AND MUSHROOM PIE

Preparation time: 30 minutes
+ 55 minutes cooking

Makes about a 1 kg (2 lb) pie

375 g (12 oz) puff pastry

125 g (4 oz) flat mushrooms

500 g (1 lb) minced beef

50 g (2 oz) fresh brown
breadcrumbs

100 ml (3 fl oz) red wine

1 tablespoon tomato purée

4 tablespoons mushroom
ketchup

1 egg, beaten

½ teaspoon salt

½ teaspoon freshly ground
black pepper

1 tablespoon finely chopped
onion

1 tablespoon semolina

beaten egg, or milk, to glaze

Oven temperatures:
Gas Mark 7/220°C/425°F
Gas Mark 4/180°C/350°F

1

2

A good old-fashioned recipe, this, of beef, mushrooms and mushroom ketchup in pastry. Here the bottom layer is pre-baked and the top layer is in strips, to ensure the pastry is cooked and the contents are not too soggy. Marvellous when cold but not chilled, this pie has proven terrifically popular when hot, too.

Preheat the oven to the first setting. Roll out just under one-third of the pastry to an oblong 28 × 18 cm (11 × 7 inches); put this on a wetted baking tray, prick it all over with a fork and bake it in the oven for 10–15 minutes.

Chop the mushroom stems finely and mix them with the beef, breadcrumbs, wine, tomato purée, 2 tablespoons of the ketchup, egg, seasoning and onion. When the cooked base has cooled, sprinkle the semolina over it and mound the meat mixture on top, leaving a border of about 1 cm (½ inch) all around. Slice the mushroom caps thickly, arrange the slices on top of the meat and sprinkle on the remaining mushroom ketchup. Roll out the remaining pastry and cut it into strips about 25 cm (10 inches) long and 2.5 cm (1 inch) wide. Lay the strips across the meat, giving them a couple of twists as you do so (illustration 1), and secure them under the cooked base by dampening the ends and pressing firmly (illustration 2). Glaze the pastry with beaten egg or milk and bake in the oven for 10 minutes. Reduce the oven temperature to the second setting and continue baking for a further 35–40 minutes, or until you are sure that the pastry on top is cooked through. Cover with greaseproof paper after about 20 minutes, to prevent drying. Serve warm or cold.

RABBIT AND PORK PIE WITH GIN AND LEMON

Preparation time: 40 minutes
+ 1¾ hours cooking + cooling

Makes about a 1.25 kg (2½ lb) pie

---

250 g (8 oz) boneless rabbit meat, cubed

1 generous tablespoon Dijon mustard

6 juniper berries, crushed

500 g (1 lb) minced pork

250 g (8 oz) unsmoked bacon

4 tablespoons gin

1 teaspoon finely grated lemon zest

2 tablespoons chopped parsley

1 quantity of hot-water pastry (page 15)

beaten egg, to glaze

1 packet of aspic powder

300 ml (½ pint) water

Oven temperatures:
Gas Mark 6/200°C/400°F
Gas Mark 4/180°C/350°F

*Rabbit and Pork Pie
with Gin and Lemon*

Prettily pale pink in colour and clean in flavour – in contrast to the richness usually associated with raised pies – this is particularly good for hot summer days or for buffets where you know the room will be hot.

Preheat the oven to the first setting. Put the rabbit into a bowl with the mustard and juniper berries; stir until the pieces are coated. Process the minced pork with the bacon and then stir in half the gin, with the lemon zest and parsley. Line the base of a 1 kg (2 lb) loaf tin with greaseproof paper and then line the whole tin with three-quarters of the pastry, keeping the remainder wrapped in a warm place until required. Stir the rabbit pieces into the minced meat mixture and press the mixture into the lined tin. Cover with a pastry lid made from the rolled-out, reserved pastry. Seal and crimp the edges firmly. Slash the top several times and pull back the pastry so the holes do not close during cooking. Put the tin on a baking tray and bake it for 30 minutes; glaze with the beaten egg and then reduce to the second setting and continue cooking for a further 1¼ hours.

Make up the aspic powder using 300 ml (½ pint) water; add the remaining gin and pour the liquid slowly into the cool pie. Once set, wrap the pie and store it in a cool place for several days before you cut it.

Pheasant, Walnut and Port Pie

Mallard Pie with Chicken and Cognac

25

MALLARD PIE WITH CHICKEN AND COGNAC

Preparation time: 1¼ hours   Makes about a 1 kg (2 lb) pie
+ 30 minutes marinating + 1¾ hours cooking + cooling

1 mallard

4 tablespoons cognac, plus extra (optional)

250 g (8 oz) minced veal

1 boneless chicken breast, minced

½ teaspoon dried thyme

½ teaspoon ground allspice

¼ teaspoon ground cloves

1 quantity of hot-water pastry (page 15)

beaten egg, to glaze

a little oil, if necessary

water

1 packet of aspic powder

Oven temperatures:
Gas Mark 6/200°C/400°F
Gas Mark 4/180°C/350°F

This is one of the best ways I know of making a single wild duck go a long way and of really enjoying its flavour into the bargain.

First pick over the mallard and remove any remaining feathers. Cut off and discard the tail. Carefully pull the skin from the breasts and reserve it. Slice the breasts off the carcase and neatly cube them. Put them into a bowl with half the cognac and leave for 30 minutes.

Preheat the oven to the first setting. Remove all the remaining flesh and skin from the mallard and process or mince it fairly finely with the skin from the breasts. Mix with the minced veal and chicken, thyme and spices.

Line a 15 cm (6-inch), round, loose-based cake tin with three-quarters of the pastry; keep the remaining pastry wrapped in a warm place. Stir the breast meat and marinade into the minced mixture and pack into the lined tin. Cover with a pastry lid made from the reserved, rolled-out pastry and crimp the edges firmly. Make a hole and pull back the edges. Put the pie on a baking tray and bake for 30 minutes. Glaze with the beaten egg. Reduce the heat to the lower temperature and bake for 1¼ hours more.

While the pie is cooking, make a stock with the mallard carcase. First brown the bones in the oven or by frying them in a little oil. Cover them with water and then simmer for about an hour or so. Strain the stock and reduce it to 300 ml (½ pint). Dissolve the aspic in the hot stock and add the remaining cognac. If you have the taste and pocket for cognac, reduce the stock further and make up the quantity with extra cognac. When the pie has cooled, pour in the liquid slowly and in stages through the hole in the top; refrigerate until the aspic has set. Wrap the pie and store it in a cool place for a few days.

PHEASANT, WALNUT AND PORT PIE

Preparation time: 1¼ hours
+ up to 3 hours cooking + cooling

Makes about a 1.5 kg (3½ lb) pie

1 cock pheasant

325 ml (11 fl oz) port

500 g (1 lb) minced pork

500 g (1 lb) minced veal

125 g (4 oz) unsmoked bacon, minced

50 g (2 oz) walnuts, chopped coarsely

2 teaspoons dried thyme

1 teaspoon ground allspice

1 teaspoon salt

2 quantities of hot-water pastry (page 15)

beaten egg, to glaze

oil for frying

water

2 packets of aspic powder

Oven temperatures:
Gas Mark 6/200°C/400°F
Gas Mark 3/160°C/325°F

This is, purposely, bigger than the other raised pie recipes, mainly to get the best value from the pheasant and extend its flavour as far as possible. The combination of pheasant with walnuts and port was specially chosen so the pie would be suitable for Christmas; but if you use frozen pheasant you can make this at any time of the year. Don't use vintage port, unless you have some opened that is in danger of not being drunk; sweet red wines made in Cyprus (Cyprus ruby wine) or British port give excellent results. Made several days in advance, such a pie makes a great show and a welcome change of pace and flavour on Boxing Day or on New Year's Eve.

First take time and care to remove what feathers and parts of feathers remain on the pheasant. Then pull off all the skin and the yellow fat you can and reserve them. Cut the breasts off the pheasant (illustration 1), slice each into four or five long strips (illustration 2), put them into a shallow dish and pour over 2 tablespoons of port. Leave to marinate for 20–30 minutes.

Preheat the oven to the first setting. Finely process all the remaining flesh and the reserved skin and fat from the pheasant; mix with the other minced meats, nuts, 3 tablespoons of the port, the thyme, allspice and salt.

Line a 25 cm (10-inch), loose-based cake tin, using three-quarters of the pastry; wrap the remaining pastry and keep it warm until needed. Put half the minced meat mixture into the lined tin and then make a layer of the strips of breast meat and cover it with the rest of the minced meat. Roll out a lid for the pie; seal and crimp the edges firmly and deeply. Slash the top and pull back the cut edges. Place the pie on a baking tray and bake it for 30 minutes. Reduce the oven to the second temperature and continue cooking for a further 2¼–2½ hours. After an hour, glaze with the beaten egg.

Meanwhile, make a rich stock by first browning the pheasant bones in a hot oven or frying them in oil. Cover the bones with water and simmer for an hour or so. Strain the liquid and reduce it to 250 ml (8 fl oz). Dissolve the aspic in the warm stock and then add the remaining port. When the cooked pie has cooled, pour in the liquid aspic slowly and in stages; refrigerate the pie until set. The pie is best left for several days before you cut it.

FISH AND SEAFOOD

SMOKED COD'S ROE PÂTÉ WITH GARLIC AND PARSLEY CHEESE

Preparation time: 5 minutes + chilling   Serves 2–4

125 g (4 oz) smoked cod's roe, skinned

78 g (2.75 oz) package of full-fat cheese with fine garlic and parsley

25 g (1 oz) butter, softened, plus extra if necessary

1 teaspoon finely grated lemon rind

lemon juice, to taste

salt and pepper

A simply made pâté with an unexpectedly full flavour that is a welcome change from the ever-popular taramasalata, which is also made with cod's roe (although traditional taramasalata is made with the roe of the Mediterranean grey mullet). The recipe can easily be doubled.

Blend the ingredients together until smooth and season. If the paste seems a little strong for your taste, add about an extra teaspoon of softened butter. Pot, cover and chill thoroughly.
   Note: If fresh roe is not available, use a 100 g (3½ oz) can and a little less cheese.

BLACK-PEPPERED SMOKED MACKEREL PÂTÉ

Preparation time: 10 minutes + chilling   Serves 6

2 fillets of peppered smoked mackerel, skinned

250 g (8 oz) skimmed milk soft cheese

150 ml (5 fl oz) carton of soured cream

1 teaspoon smooth Dijon mustard

The popularity of smoked mackerel fillets coated with coarsely ground black pepper inspired me to make something sharper and more interesting than run-of-the-mill mackerel pâtés. It was successful enough to be made twice on the same day.

Mash the fish in a bowl with a fork, and then gradually beat the fish into the cheese. Add the soured cream and mustard and continue beating the mixture until it is very well blended. You can use a food processor if you prefer, but take great care not to over-process the mixture: it should retain some texture and not be smooth. Pack the pâté into a decorative bowl or individual dishes. Cover and chill thoroughly before serving with very good bread or rolls.

POTTED SMOKED TROUT WITH MUSTARD

Preparation time: 10 minutes + chilling   Serves 4–6

175 g (6 oz) smoked trout
fillets

1–2 teaspoons Dijon
mustard

125 g (4 oz) unsalted
butter, softened

Quickly made, this relies on the traditional friendship of smoked foods with mustard.

Process half the trout fillets, 1 teaspoon of the mustard and the butter until smooth. Add the remaining fish and process in two or three short bursts, so that there are still discernible pieces of fish. Do not over-process. Taste, and stir in the extra mustard if liked. Serve chilled, but not directly from the refrigerator.

SMOKED SALMON PÂTÉ

Preparation time: 15 minutes + chilling   Serves 6–8

250 g (8 oz) smoked salmon

175 g (6 oz) salted butter,
plus extra to seal

lemon juice, to taste

1 tablespoon cognac or dry
white vermouth

150 ml (5 fl oz) carton of
double cream, whipped
lightly

a little white pepper

To garnish:

a sprig of fresh dill or a little
dried dill (optional)

Although smoked salmon is used here, this is the base recipe for making a pâté from any ready-to-eat fish, especially an expensive one which you would like to go further. Smoked trout and prawns are particularly good.

It is pointless making a smoked salmon pâté that is cooked, for many of the delicate nuances of flavour will be lost. This richly flavoured and textured pâté relies on the natural partnership of fish with butter and cream; while stretching a small amount of smoked salmon a very long way, it nevertheless allows the salmon's flavour to sparkle through. Very simple to make either in smaller quantities or multiplied several times for parties. At the end of the recipe are some ideas for grand occasion serving.

Cut the salmon into small pieces. Heat the butter over a gentle heat and remove immediately from the heat once it has melted. Pour it into a liquidiser or food processor, add the salmon and process until the mixture is very smooth. Add a little lemon juice, white pepper and the cognac or dry white vermouth and mix through. Scoop the mixture into a bowl and allow to cool to room temperature without beginning to set. Fold in the cream evenly and lightly. Scoop the pâté into individual ramekins or one larger, attractive container.

When the pâté is set and thoroughly chilled, seal the top with a little melted butter, and perhaps decorate it with a sprig of fresh dill or a sprinkle of dried dill.

VARIATIONS

- Fresh summer herbs can be blended into the pâté with care: try dill weed, tarragon, thyme, fennel or even parsley.
- Fresh lime juice is a fascinating alternative to lemon juice.
- Vodka will give extra but subtle and unrecognised flavour.
- Instead of passing the pâté around with toast, scoop it into pretty shapes and serve with a mixture of salad leaves on a flat plate, to be eaten with a fork or a knife and fork. Dress the lot with a subtle dressing of light oil and citrus juice, or with vodka flavoured with lime juice or merely with chilled hazelnut or walnut oil and a light grating of lemon or lime zest over each serving.
- Once the mixture has set, it is perfect as a stuffing for vegetables or cooked fish and can even be piped if it is not too cold. It is superb on thick slices of cucumber or in celery boats. If you can run to an extra 25–50 g (1–2 oz) of smoked salmon per person, roll or fold the slices around the pâté to make parcels or cushions. This is especially effective if you make a prawn pâté and wrap that in smoked salmon.
- It is just as effective to line small ramekins or baked pastry boats with smoked salmon slices before adding the pâté.
- Texture and added interest in flavour and appearance can be given by folding in extra chopped smoked salmon or some other fish, notably coarsely chopped prawns.

POTTED COGNAC HERRING ROES IN SMOKED SALMON

Preparation time: 10 minutes + chilling   Serves 2–3

125 g (4 oz) can of soft herring roes, drained

75 g (3 oz) butter, softened

a generous pinch of ground mace

2 teaspoons cognac

3 thin slices of smoked salmon

salt and freshly ground black pepper

To serve:

lettuce leaves

slices of lemon

The rich paste of soft herring roes is delicious served as it is with hot toast, as a snack or first course. Here it is given dinner party status with a smart wrap of smoked salmon. The recipe is easily doubled or trebled. Serve two or three rolls per person, according to how you garnish them and what is to follow.

Process the roes with the butter, mace and cognac. Season with a little salt and pepper, transfer to a small bowl, cover, and chill for at least an hour.

Cut each slice of salmon in half, to give six strips about 10 × 5 cm (4 × 2 inches). Put a sixth of the herring mixture on the bottom of each strip and form into a rough sausage shape. Roll up the smoked salmon to form neat rolls. Cover and chill for several hours. Serve with lettuce leaves and slices of lemon.

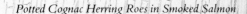

Potted Cognac Herring Roes in Smoked Salmon

Smoked Salmon Pâté, served in smoked-salmon-lined pastry boats

Smoked Mackerel Pâté with Red Beans, Beetroot and Horseradish

33

SMOKED MACKEREL PÂTÉ WITH RED BEANS, BEETROOT AND HORSERADISH

Preparation time: 10 minutes + chilling   Serves 6–12

175 g (6 oz) smoked mackerel fillets, skinned

400 g (14 oz) canned red kidney beans, rinsed and drained

40 g (1½ oz) pickled beetroot

1–2 teaspoons creamed horseradish

150 ml (5 fl oz) carton of soured cream

To serve (optional):

radicchio leaves

chopped parsley

olive oil

garlic

With its super rosy-pink colour and slight bite of pickled beetroot and horseradish, this light pâté is deliciously different, and particularly welcome when you have to make a variety of fish-based pâtés for a buffet.

Process the fish, 125 g (4 oz) of the beans and the beetroot until you have a fairly smooth paste. Stir in 1 teaspoon of horseradish and fold through the soured cream, taking care not to overbeat. Taste and add more horseradish, if necessary. Cover and chill.

For dinner parties, it is interesting to serve the pâté scooped into radicchio leaves to echo the colour. Use the remainder of the beans to make a salad with lots of chopped parsley, olive oil and garlic, and arrange everything together on individual plates.

NO-BAKE FISH TERRINE

Preparation time: 30 minutes + chilling   Serves 6 or more

500 g (1 lb) boneless white fish

250 g (8 oz) boneless smoked fish

125 g (4 oz) cooked, drained, chopped spinach

300 ml (½ pint) medium-dry or slightly sweet white wine, plus extra if necessary

25 g (1 oz) shallot or onion, chopped

15 g (½ oz) parsley stalks

2 strips of orange peel

1 strip of lemon peel

Any fish with a good rich flavour can be used as the base for this terrine; the flavour will be preserved because it is not baked for ages. Whiting is especially good for the white fish and although it would be more usual to use a more expensive fish, say salmon, as the second choice, there is no reason why you could not reverse the combination, or combine two expensive fish: a salmon terrine with veins of monkfish, or monkfish with prawns, and so on. If choosing a smoked fish, make sure it does not have added colour or you will get very strange results indeed. Naturally-smoked haddock is probably the best choice; kippers have too many bones to remove successfully. Once you have decided, give the terrine whatever name you like. It is always important when using wine with fish that the wine should be slightly sweet.

a dried bay leaf
12 black peppercorns, crushed
2 egg whites
11 g (⅓ oz) envelope of gelatine
a little lemon juice, if necessary
oil for greasing
salt, pepper and nutmeg

Check all the fish for skin and bones. Check again that the spinach has been squeezed dry of all moisture and season it fairly highly with salt, pepper and nutmeg, remembering that these seasonings are needed to flavour almost three times that volume eventually.

Put the white fish, wine, shallot or onion, parsley stalks, orange and lemon peel, bay leaf and peppercorns into a pan and bring to the boil as slowly as you can; poach gently until the fish flakes. Remove the white fish and poach the smoked fish in the same stock. Drain off the stock and measure its volume. You will need 150 ml (¼ pint) of stock, so make it up by adding more white wine or reduce it over a gentle heat.

Process the spinach, egg whites and white fish. Dissolve the gelatine powder over a gentle heat in a little of the stock, ensuring that it is fully dissolved. Blend with the remaining stock and stir into the fish and spinach mixture. Now is the time to adjust the seasoning, perhaps adding a little more lemon juice, but don't lose the flavour of the fish.

Lightly oil a 900 ml (1½-pint) container, or line it with cling film (although this can give a distinctly crinkled appearance). Spoon in slightly more than half of the spinach mixture; then arrange the second fish on top, cut or pulled into long strips. Add the rest of the mixture, smooth the top, cover and leave the flavours to develop while it sets.

VARIATIONS

- Instead of using smoked fish for the central layer, you could use ready-cooked prawns or mussels, or drained and rinsed smoked oysters or clams; the latter won't need poaching of course.
- You can also make a fish and vegetable terrine, with lightly, poached asparagus stems down the centre perhaps.
- Try a mixture of poached salmon flakes and cooked, shelled quails' eggs.

TERRINE OF WHITING WITH TARRAGON

Preparation time: 10 minutes + 1 hour   Serves 6–8
chilling + 40–50 minutes cooking + chilling

750 g (1½ lb) whiting or
plaice fillets, skinned

2 egg whites

125 g (4 oz) fromage frais

150 ml (¼ pint) carton of
double cream

1 teaspoon salt

½ teaspoon ground white
pepper

3 tablespoons white wine

1 teaspoon dried tarragon,
plus extra if wished

butter, for greasing

Oven temperature:
Gas Mark 4/180°C/350°F

*This recipe is the essential 'blueprint' for any number
of fish-based, mousse-like terrines. Whiting and plaice
are both especially good for it, as they retain their
flavour.*

Chop 500 g (1 lb) of the fish and put it into a food
processor. Process briefly; then add the egg
whites and process again. Add the fromage frais,
cream, salt and pepper and process until fairly
smooth. Chill for at least an hour.

Preheat the oven. Put the wine and tarragon
into a small pan and heat gently until the wine
bubbles. Allow to cool completely. Strain one
tablespoon of the tarragon-flavoured wine into
the fish mixture.

Butter a 750 ml (1¼-pint) capacity terrine and
make a layer of half the fish mixture. Lay half of
the remaining fillets on top and sprinkle with the
wine and tarragon mixture. Repeat with the rest
of the fish fillets and wine and finish with the
other half of the fish purée. Cover with a lid or
foil and place in a bain-marie; bake in the oven
for 40–50 minutes. Let it cool completely in the
tin so that the liquid can be reabsorbed.

This is nice with a well flavoured mayonnaise,
perhaps with extra tarragon, or with a dollop of
soured cream.

Terrine of Whiting with Tarragon
Salmon and Wild Mushroom Terrine

SALMON AND WILD MUSHROOM TERRINE

Preparation time: 45 minutes + 45 minutes cooking   Serves 6–8

25 g (1 oz) butter

50 g (2 oz) onion, chopped finely

2 garlic cloves, crushed

175 g (6 oz) wild mushrooms or flat field mushrooms, wiped and sliced thickly if necessary

10 cm (4-inch) piece of cucumber, de-seeded and cut into thick matchsticks

4 tablespoons dry white wine

1 kg (2 lb) fresh salmon, cut into escalopes

plain flour

1 tablespoon oil

150 g (5 oz) basmati rice, rinsed

2 eggs

150 ml (¼ pint) milk

150 ml (5 fl oz) carton of double cream

½ teaspoon salt

½ teaspoon ground nutmeg

4 hard-boiled eggs, shelled

freshly ground black pepper

Oven temperature:
Gas Mark 4/180°C/350°F

Preheat the oven. Melt half the butter in a saucepan and in it cook the onion and garlic over a gentle heat until the onion is soft but not browned. Add the mushrooms and plenty of freshly ground black pepper; cook for 2 minutes. Add the cucumber and wine and cook over a moderate heat until it is reduced to a glaze.

Toss the salmon escalopes in flour and shake off any surplus. Heat the remaining butter with the oil in a frying pan and cook the salmon briefly on both sides, just to seal; do not over-cook. Cook the rice in plenty of boiling, salted water for 12–15 minutes until cooked *al dente*; drain.

Mix together the eggs, milk and cream. Season this custard with the salt, nutmeg and more pepper.

Line a loaf tin or terrine with cling film. Use half the salmon to make a layer on the bottom of the terrine; cover with half the sliced hard-boiled eggs. Add half the mushroom mixture and cover with half the rice. Repeat the layers ending with rice; then pour over the custard.

Stand the terrine in a bain-marie and bake for 45 minutes. This is nice with soured cream and chopped dill.

SMOKED COD BRANDADE

Preparation and cooking time: 15 minutes   Serves 6 or more

250 g (8 oz) smoked cod
fillet, skinned

20 g (¾ oz) butter

1 clove of garlic, peeled and
chopped finely

125 g (4 oz) peeled potato,
sliced

125 ml (4 fl oz) milk

150 ml (5 fl oz) olive oil, at
room temperature

white pepper and salt
(optional)

To serve:

crudités

crusty bread

True brandade de morue, a speciality of the south of France, is made from salted cod, takes ages, and if the cod has not been soaked properly can be foul beyond belief. This version is a cinch to make and, although meant to be eaten cold as a type of spreading pâté, is so good when warm that you will have trouble saving enough of it to cool.

Put the fish in a bowl and cover it with boiling water. Melt the butter in a saucepan, add the garlic and potato, pour the milk over and bring to the boil. Simmer very gently, covered, for 6–8 minutes, until the potatoes are just beginning to soften. Drain the fish and put it on top of the potatoes, cover again and continue to simmer for a further 5–6 minutes, until the fish begins to flake.

Put everything into the food processor and process to a paste. With the motor running, add the oil in a steady trickle, as you do for mayonnaise, until it has all been incorporated and you have a light, creamy mixture. Season the brandade with a little white pepper and a touch of salt if you like; don't overdo the salt as smoked fish usually makes it salty enough. Serve it warm or cold with crudités and crusty bread.

AN ANDALUCIAN ASPIC OF PAELLA

Preparation and cooking time: 1 hour
+ several hours chilling

Serves 6–8

175 g (6 oz) canned cooked squid or baby octopus
200 ml (7 fl oz) sweet white wine
½ teaspoon salt
6 black peppercorns
1 bay leaf
2 or 3 parsley stalks
1 garlic clove, chopped
125 g (4 oz) cooked shelled mussels
125 g (4 oz) cooked shelled prawns
½ small red pepper
25 g (1 oz) long grain rice
a generous handful of coarsely chopped fresh parsley
1 or 2 sachets of powdered saffron, according to taste
2 packets of aspic powder

Paella is Andalucia's equivalent of the Sunday joint. Based on ancient styles of cooking, it combines poultry, seafood and vegetables with saffron rice. Here, just seafood is used to make a superbly colourful and tasty reminder of Spanish sojourns.

Cut the squid into 1 cm (½-inch) rings; leave the baby octopuses whole. Pour over the wine, add the salt, peppercorns, bay leaf, parsley stalks and garlic and simmer gently for 2 minutes. Add the mussels and prawns and turn off the heat immediately. Allow to cool. Strain, and reserve the liquid.

Cut the pepper into thin, even strips and blanch these for 1 minute in boiling water; drain and refresh them under cold running water, and pat dry. Cook the rice in boiling, salted water until tender but not soggy; drain it and spread it out on a plate to steam dry. Stir the parsley into the cooked rice, with the pepper strips. Make up the reserved cooking liquid to 750 ml (1¼ pints) with water, add the saffron powder, sprinkle over the aspic powder and heat gently, stirring until dissolved. Stir the seafood into the rice mixture, discarding the bay leaf and other seasonings.

Rinse a 1 kg (2 lb) loaf tin with cold water and pour in enough aspic liquid to cover the bottom. Chill until set. Spoon in half the rice mixture and pour over half the liquid. Chill until just beginning to set but not yet firm. Carefully spoon in the remaining mixture, giving the tin a shake and several taps to ensure that the liquid penetrates thoroughly. Chill until set. Unmould and serve in slices, perhaps with a garlic mayonnaise spiked with a dash of hot paprika.

An Andalucian Aspic of Paella

PORK AND GAME

POTTED GROUSE WITH COGNAC

Preparation time: 1½ hours
+ 45 minutes cooking + chilling

Makes about 375 g (12 oz)

1 grouse, dressed

50 g (2 oz) smoked streaky bacon

25 g (1 oz) butter

25 g (1 oz) onion, sliced

½ small bay leaf

1 small garlic clove

600 ml (1 pint) strong red wine

125 g (4 oz) fatty belly of pork, sliced

6 black peppercorns

3 whole allspice berries

cognac

a little melted butter

Just one grouse will make a tantalisingly flavoured pâté for six or more people with this method. Naturally, the older the bird, the better the flavour. It might be as well to unwrap a fresh bird and let it sit in a cool place for a few days. Frozen grouse work just as well, of course.

Cut the grouse in half. Slice the bacon into small pieces and put these, with the butter and onion, in a small pan. Cook until the onion is starting to soften and the bacon fat is rendering. Add the grouse and cook gently until nicely browned here and there: say 10 minutes. Now add the bay leaf, garlic, red wine, belly of pork and spices, bring to the boil and simmer until the grouse flesh falls from the bones; this will probably take 45 minutes, more if an older bird.

Take the halves of grouse from the liquid and put them aside to cool. Reduce the contents of the pan until only 4 tablespoons of liquid remain. Take all the flesh from the cooked grouse off the bones and add, with the contents of the pan, to a liquidiser or food processor. Process until fairly smooth. Add cognac to taste and then spoon into a suitable bowl. Chill; then seal with a little melted butter. Wrap and store in a cool place for at least 24 hours. Serve with toast or hot rolls.

ALMOND-POTTED PARTRIDGE WITH WHITE GRAPES

Preparation time: 10 minutes
+ 40 minutes cooking + chilling

Makes about 375 g (12 oz)

1 partridge, dressed

300 ml (½ pint) good-quality white wine

25 g (1 oz) onion, chopped very finely

½ small bay leaf

2.5 cm (1-inch) long, 1 cm (½-inch) wide strip of lemon peel

2 juniper berries

125 g (4 oz) unsalted butter, plus a little extra

4 tablespoons double cream

50 g (2 oz) ground almonds

½ teaspoon salt

1 tablespoon cognac (optional)

50–125 g (2–4 oz) seedless white grapes

a little butter, melted

a little nutmeg

white pepper (optional)

The delicate sweetness of partridge breast is easily swamped by other flavours. However, gently poached in white wine and complemented by seedless white grapes, with unsalted butter and ground almonds, its taste triumphs; this is an excellent way to stretch such a treat to be shared by up to six people.

Cut the partridge into four pieces and place these in a small saucepan. Add the wine, onion, bay leaf, lemon peel and juniper berries. Cover and simmer gently until the flesh is falling from the bones, about 40 minutes. Remove the partridge pieces, strain the liquid and reduce to about 4 tablespoons.

Melt the butter and pour it into a liquidiser with the cream, partridge flesh, reduced stock and ground almonds. Reduce to a very smooth purée and season with salt and a little nutmeg. Add white pepper if you need that, too. Mix in the cognac if you are convinced the flavour will not be too strong.

Wash and dry the grapes; if they are large, cut them in half. (If you cannot get seedless grapes, halve and de-seed others.) Fold the grapes into the mixture, assessing by eye the right amount: they should not dominate; merely punctuate. Spoon into a suitable container and chill, covering with a little melted butter to seal.

This is ideal for serving in scoops on small plates or in small bowls, with an unusual salad dressed with a nut oil, or with a very special hot toast or buns – brioches perhaps.

VARIATION

● A small, sweet hen pheasant could be prepared like this, and so could a guinea-fowl.

VENISON PÂTÉ WITH CARAMELISED CHESTNUTS

Preparation time: 15 minutes
+ 1 hour cooking

Makes about 1.2 kg (2¾ lb)

---

375 g (12 oz) venison neck fillet

2 tablespoons cognac

3 teaspoons white wine vinegar

25 g (1 oz) white sugar

25 g (1 oz) butter

475 g (15 oz) can of cooked whole chestnuts, drained

375 g (12 oz) minced veal

250 g (8 oz) minced pork

50 g (2 oz) onion, chopped finely

2 garlic cloves, chopped

1 teaspoon ground cinnamon

½ teaspoon ground nutmeg

1 teaspoon salt

Oven temperature:
Gas Mark 4/180°C/350°F

This is for those who have the contemporary taste for less highly flavoured game. A relatively small amount of high-quality venison complements an unusual combination of smoky-flavoured chestnuts and rich brown caramel. Truly delicious.

Preheat the oven. Cut half the venison into strips about 7 × 1 cm (3 × ½ inch) and spoon on the cognac and 1 teaspoon of white wine vinegar. Cook the sugar and butter together until they are a really rich brown but not burnt; add the remaining 2 teaspoons of vinegar and 125 g (4 oz) of the whole chestnuts and agitate the pan gently until the chestnuts are well covered and the sauce is smooth. Keep warm.

Mash the remaining chestnuts and mince the rest of the venison. Put in a large bowl with the minced veal and pork and mix thoroughly together, with the onion, garlic, spices and salt. Carefully pour the excess caramel from the pan into the mixture and mix thoroughly. Fold in the whole chestnuts, trying not to break them up.

Pack half the mixture into a 900 ml (1½-pint) loaf tin. Arrange the marinated venison lengthways and sprinkle on any marinade which has not been absorbed. Cover with the remaining veal mixture and mound it up slightly to give a nice shape.

Place in a bain-marie and bake for about an hour or until the juices run clear. Cool, wrap and store for at least 24 hours before serving with sharp fruit or fruit jellies, such as redcurrant.

Almond-Potted Partridge with
White Grapes

Pigeon Pâté with Orange
and Hazelnuts

Venison Pâté with Caramelised
Chestnuts

45

PIGEON PÂTÉ WITH ORANGE AND HAZELNUTS

Preparation time: 1 hour + 1¼ hours cooking   Makes about 500 g (1 lb)
+ cooling and pressing

2 pigeons

1 teaspoon finely grated
orange rind

2 garlic cloves, crushed

3 tablespoons cognac

1 tablespoon oil, plus extra
for greasing

150 g (5 oz) onion, chopped
finely

1 bay leaf

1 sprig of fresh thyme or a
pinch of dried thyme

6 black peppercorns

water

125 g (4 oz) streaky bacon,
without rind

375 g (12 oz) minced pork

2 tablespoons chopped
hazelnuts, roasted

½ teaspoon ground nutmeg

salt and freshly ground black
pepper

Oven temperature:
Gas Mark 3/160°C/325°F

*Pigeon breasts are marinated with orange and cognac
and baked in the middle of a pork pâté, which is
flavoured with a greatly reduced stock made from the
birds' bones. This way, you get far more flavour from
just two pigeons than is normally possible.*

Remove the breasts from the pigeons; slice the
breasts thinly and put into a shallow dish with
the orange rind, garlic and cognac. Leave to
marinate for as long as it takes for the next stage
to be completed.

Heat the oil and nicely brown half the onion
with the pigeon carcases. Add the bay leaf,
thyme and peppercorns and barely cover with
water. Cover, bring to the boil and then simmer
for at least 1 hour. Strain, return the stock to the
pan and reduce over high heat until only 6 tablespoons remain. Preheat the oven.

Mix together the bacon, pork and remaining
onion; add the hazelnuts, nutmeg, seasonings
and reduced stock. Press half the mixture into an
oiled 500 g (1 lb) loaf tin; make a layer of the
marinated pigeon breast slices evenly along the
mixture and dribble on any remaining marinade.
Cover with the remaining pork mixture. Put the
tin into a bain-marie and bake for 1¼ hours.

Once cool but not cold, put a 500 g (1 lb) pack
of lentils, rice or something similar on top,
moulding it to the pâté's shape. Allow to
become quite cold in the tin before turning out.
Keep refrigerated but bring to just below room
temperature before serving. A Cumberland
sauce, or any sauce that is made with berries and
has a distinct sharpness, would be an excellent
accompaniment; so would a whole-grain
mustard that had some elegance.

A PARTY PÂTÉ OF VENISON

Preparation time: 24 hours marinating
+ 30 minutes + 2½ hours cooking + cooling   Makes about 1.35 kg (3¼ lb)

500 g (1 lb) lean stewing
venison

300 ml (½ pint) full-bodied
red wine

50 g (2 oz) onion, chopped

2 garlic cloves, chopped

1 orange, weighing about
125 g (4 oz), de-seeded and
sliced

8 juniper berries, crushed

12 black peppercorns

1 large dried bay leaf

2 blades of mace

2 teaspoons ground
cinnamon

½ teaspoon ground nutmeg

250 g (8 oz) smoked streaky
bacon

1 teaspoon dried thyme

½ teaspoon dried rosemary

500 g (1 lb) chicken livers,
puréed

250 g (8 oz) minced pork

2 tablespoons cognac

50 g (2 oz) ground almonds

25 g (1 oz) dried white
breadcrumbs (optional)

Oven temperature:
Gas Mark 4/180°C/350°F

A big, highly flavoured pâté is just the thing to have around on holiday weekends, especially over Christmas and the New Year, and the increased availability of venison makes this the ideal choice. In contrast to the recipe for Venison with Caramelised Chestnuts (page 44), it uses cheaper, more flavoursome cuts, and includes the traditional accompaniments to venison, to increase the effect. This is the sort of rich flavour really appreciated on cold days, especially if you are eating outdoors.

Cut the venison into small pieces and put to marinate with the wine, onion, garlic, orange slices, juniper berries, peppercorns, bay leaf, mace, cinnamon and nutmeg. Leave for 24 hours in a cool but not cold place, turning from time to time.

Cut up the bacon, add that to the venison and its marinade and cook the entirety at a gentle simmer until the venison is tender, about 1½ hours, by which time most of the fat of the bacon should have been rendered into the mixture. Remove the pieces of meat and add the thyme and rosemary to the cooking liquid. Strain, reserving the pan contents, and reduce it to just less than 150 ml (¼ pint).

Preheat the oven. Make a purée of everything left in the pan, including the orange slices, leaving just a little texture. Stir in the puréed chicken livers and minced pork. Mix in the reduced stock, cognac and ground almonds. If you would like a really firm pâté for slicing, also stir in the breadcrumbs.

Spoon half the pâté into an oval baking dish of about 1.75-litre (3-pint) capacity; add the venison and bacon in a layer and spread the remaining pâté on top. Stand the dish in a bain-marie and bake for about an hour or until the juices no longer run pink. Allow to cool and then store, well wrapped, for at least 24 hours before cutting.

SWEDISH LIVER PUDDING

Preparation time: 25 minutes
+ 35 minutes cooking + cooling

Makes about 875 g (1¾ lb)

---

500 g (1 lb) pig's liver

250 g (8 oz) minced pork

175 g (6 oz) long grain rice

300 ml (½ pint) milk

3 tablespoons seedless
raisins or currants

2 tablespoons molasses or
black treacle

1 teaspoon salt

1 teaspoon fresh thyme
leaves or ½ teaspoon dried
thyme

½ teaspoon ground allspice

2 eggs, beaten

oil for greasing

Oven temperature:
Gas Mark 5/190°C/375°F

---

*Unusual as it sounds, this recipe makes a truly
delicious pâté that, baked in a round tin, looks and cuts
like a cake. The inclusion of both rice and treacle gives
a rich smooth flavour, clearly planned to placate those
who don't usually like pork liver.*

Preheat the oven. In the food processor or
mincer, make a smooth or lightly textured paste
of the liver and pork. Cook the rice in the milk,
tightly covered, over a very low heat, for
12 minutes, when the liquid will have been
absorbed and the rice will be tender. Into the
warm, cooked rice, stir the raisins or currants,
molasses or treacle, salt, thyme, allspice and
beaten eggs; add the meat mixture and beat well.

Spoon into a greased 18 cm (7-inch) loose-
bottomed cake tin and bake for 30–35 minutes,
until brown on top and firm to touch. Cool in
the tin before turning out. Serve cut in thin
wedges with a well flavoured sauce: I would add
grated orange rind or cognac to a redcurrant
sauce.

VARIATION

- Substitute chicken or turkey livers for pig's
  liver.
- Replace the raisins or currants with small
  white seedless raisins.

THE ESSENTIAL PORK-BASED PÂTÉ

Preparation time: 10 minutes
+ 1–1¾ hours cooking + pressing (optional)

Makes about 1 kg (2 lb)

500 g (1 lb) minced pork

500 g (1 lb) minced veal

250 g (8 oz) smoked streaky bacon, minced finely

150 ml (¼ pint) dry white wine

2 large garlic cloves, chopped

1 teaspoon dried thyme

1 teaspoon dried rosemary

3 tablespoons chopped fresh parsley, including stalks

2 tablespoons dried white breadcrumbs

black or white pepper, to taste

Oven temperature:
Gas Mark 3/160°C/325°F

This is not so much a recipe but the specifications for you to develop your own style of pork-based pâté. By varying the proportions of each of the main ingredients, you will alter both flavour and appearance. The inclusion of breadcrumbs is good home-cookery practice, because it ensures that more of the juices are retained without the bore of pressing. The recipe can easily be halved.

Preheat the oven. Mix together the pork, veal and bacon and stir in the remaining ingredients; it is important that your dried herbs are very fresh, especially the rosemary. Use a light touch, so that the texture of the meats is not affected too much. Transfer to a 1 kg (2 lb) loaf tin or two 500 g (1 lb) loaf tins. Stand the tin(s) in a bain-marie and bake in the oven for 1½–1¾ hours for the large pâté, 1–1¼ hours for the smaller versions.

If you would like to press the pâtés, let them cool to room temperature and then lay on top of them one or two packets of rice, lentils or something similar that can be moulded to the shape of the pâté. Store well wrapped in foil. This pâté is best left for 24 hours or more before cutting.

VARIATIONS

- This sort of pâté is commonly cooked in a wrapping of bacon. If cooking in a loaf tin so that the pâté can be turned out, first line the tin with overlapping strips of streaky bacon which have been stretched with the back of a heavy kitchen knife, to stop them shrinking during cooking. If cooking in an oval dish from which the pâté can be cut, you might simply put the stretched strips over the top, tucking them well down the sides. Short rashers can be arranged to meet in the middle, long ones arranged parallel. You will need

250 g (8 oz) in most cases, and this increases both the cost and the fat content.

- For extra bite, stir in 1 or 2 teaspoons of lightly crushed green peppercorns
- Whole chicken or turkey livers, lightly browned in oil or butter, can be arranged in a central layer or folded through the mixture.
- Reconstituted dried mushrooms, thickly sliced flat mushrooms or whole button mushrooms can be added, perhaps with 1 or 2 tablespoons of mushroom ketchup. This version may make extra liquid, to which you should add a little extra white wine; then lightly thicken it with arrowroot or cornflour to serve as a cold dressing for the sliced pâté. Mixed with gelatine powder, or aspic in the usual proportions, this can also be spooned over the pâté as a sparkling outer layer.

FRENCH PORK LIVER PÂTÉ

Preparation time: 10 minutes
+ 2–2½ hours cooking + cooling

Makes 750 g (1½ lb)

500 g (1 lb) pig's liver

25 g (1 oz) onion

1 large garlic clove

250 g (8 oz) back bacon, minced

250 g (8 oz) minced pork

1 teaspoon ground nutmeg

2 tablespoons white wine

2 tablespoons cognac

freshly ground black pepper

Oven temperature:
Gas Mark 1/140°C/275°F

You love it or hate it. Those are the only possible responses to pâtés in which pig's liver is a major component. Traditionally, pâtés have been a very important way to preserve and enjoy the large livers of autumn pigs, and each pig-raising area of France has its own version. This one gives a nice rich flavour, which is helped by the very low onion content, the inclusion of fresh pork and the use of sweeter back bacon rather than streaky. Too much onion or bacon seem to make pig's liver taste stronger. The long, slow cooking also encourages a gentler flavour. You could, of course, use chicken or poultry livers instead.

Preheat the oven. Purée the liver with the onion and garlic. Mix together with the remaining ingredients, season with 5–6 turns of the peppermill and spoon into a 750 g (1½ lb) loaf tin. Seal tightly with foil, place in a bain–marie and bake in the oven for 2–2½ hours.

VEAL AND OTHER MEATS

CALVES' LIVER PÂTÉ WITH GREEN-PEPPERCORN-CARAMELISED PEARS

Preparation time: 20 minutes + chilling + 40 minutes cooking + cooling

Makes about 750 g (1½ lb)

For the mousseline:

500 g (1 lb) calves' liver

1 tablespoon finely chopped onion

½ teaspoon salt

1 teaspoon tarragon vinegar or white wine vinegar

2 eggs, beaten

150 ml (5 fl oz) carton of double cream

For the caramelised pears:

125 g (4 oz) granulated sugar

1 teaspoon tarragon vinegar or white wine vinegar

1 teaspoon green pepper-corns, rinsed and drained

oil for greasing

1 large pear, preferably a Comice

Oven temperatures:
Gas Mark 4/180°C/350°F
Gas Mark 3/160°C/325°F

This is served warm or chilled, turned out, with the richly coloured pears providing visual contrast to the mousseline. A perfect way to begin an important meal.

Purée the liver with the onion, salt, vinegar and eggs. Gradually add the cream until blended; do not over-process. Strain the mixture into a bowl, using a fine sieve and forcing the purée through with the back of a soup ladle; this speeds up the process enormously. Cover and chill in the refrigerator for at least 30 minutes.

Preheat the oven to the first setting. Make a caramel by heating the sugar in a heavy-bottomed pan, *without stirring*, until it is a rich brown liquid. Add the vinegar and peppercorns: take care, it will splutter. Stir until mixed and then pour into an oiled 18 cm (7-inch) square cake tin. Peel, core and slice the pear thinly: start slicing at the stem end and once you reach the wider base of the pear, turn it through 90° and slice across, so all the pieces are approximately the same size and shape (see illustration). Arrange the slices decoratively on the savoury caramel.

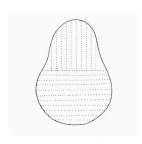

Calves' Liver Pâté with Green-Peppercorn-Caramelised Pears

Spoon the chilled liver purée over the pears, put the cake tin into a bain-marie and bake it for 10 minutes. Reduce the oven temperature to the second setting and bake for a further 30 minutes. Allow to cool in the tin for 10 minutes before turning out. Serve warm or cool, cut into squares, with a few interesting salad leaves such as slightly bitter frisé (curly endive) or radicchio. Otherwise a pool of absolutely smooth apple purée sharpened with a little tarragon vinegar and garnished with fresh tarragon would look very special.

PIMENTO, VEAL AND HAM PÂTÉ WITH CHICKEN CHUNKS

Preparation time: 10 minutes + 45 minutes cooking + cooling

Makes about 625 g (1¼ lb)

175 g (6 oz) minced veal

175 g (6 oz) cooked ham, chopped

25 g (1 oz) onion, chopped

1 small garlic clove, crushed

50 g (2 oz) canned pimento, rinsed and drained

4 eggs

2 generous tablespoons chopped fresh parsley

150 ml (5 fl oz) carton of double cream

175 g (6 oz) chicken breast, diced neatly

oil for greasing

salt and freshly ground black pepper

Oven temperature:
Gas Mark 4/180°C/350°F

A lively mixture of veal and ham, puréed with pimento and baked with chunks of white chicken breast.

Preheat the oven. Put the minced veal, ham, onion and garlic into a food processor and process until fairly smooth. Add the pimento, eggs and parsley and process for a further 30 seconds. Season with salt and pepper and gradually add the double cream, using the pulse action on the machine, until thoroughly blended; do not over-mix. Transfer to a bowl and carefully stir in the pieces of chicken breast.

Grease a 500 g (1 lb) loaf tin and spoon the mixture into it, taking care to fill all the corners and giving the tin a few sharp taps to dispel any air pockets. Cover with greased foil, stand in a bain-marie and bake for about 45 minutes, until firm to touch. Allow to cool completely in the tin before turning out.

POTTED TONGUE

Preparation time: 10 minutes + chilling | Serves 6

175 g (6 oz) cooked tongue

50 g (2 oz) cooked turkey or chicken breast meat

1 tablespoon orange marmalade

2 teaspoons cranberry or redcurrant jelly

½ teaspoon ground nutmeg

125 g (4 oz) butter, softened

clarified or concentrated butter, melted, if necessary

Put all the ingredients except the clarified or concentrated butter into a food processor and process until fairly smooth. Transfer to six little pots and chill thoroughly. If the potted tongue is to be kept for longer than 48 hours, cover the pots with a thin layer of clarified or concentrated butter.

VEAL AND CHICKEN PÂTÉ WITH CHICKEN LIVERS

Preparation time: 30 minutes + marinating + 1¼ hours cooking + cooling | Makes about 375 g (12 oz)

250 g (8 oz) chicken livers

2 tablespoons cognac

125 g (4 oz) chicken breast, minced

1 egg, beaten

3 tablespoons ground almonds

1 teaspoon allspice

salt and white pepper

Oven temperature:
Gas Mark 4/180°C/350°F

An elegant pâté, quickly made, in which the sweet, delicate flavour of veal is heightened with chicken breast; the result contrasts with the texture and fuller flavour of chicken livers perfumed with cognac.

After trimming the chicken livers and cutting off any green staining, pat them dry on kitchen paper and put half of them into a bowl. Sprinkle them with the cognac and let them stand for at least 30 minutes. Preheat the oven.

Mince the rest of the livers finely and add them to the remaining ingredients. Season generously with salt and white pepper. Pack half the mixture into a 500 g (1 lb) loaf tin. Put a layer of the marinated livers on top and then cover with the remaining mixture. Press down firmly. Stand the tin in a bain–marie and bake for 1¼ hours.

ALMOND VEAL PÂTÉ MARBLED WITH FRESH LIME GREMOLATA

Preparation time: 10 minutes
+ 40–60 minutes cooking + cooling

Makes about 625 g (1¼ lb)

500 g (1 lb) minced veal

2 eggs

150 ml (5 fl oz) carton of double cream

25 g (1 oz) ground almonds

½ teaspoon ground white pepper

½ teaspoon salt

For the gremolata:

25 g (1 oz) parsley, chopped coarsely, including stalks

2 teaspoons finely grated fresh lime zest

1–2 garlic cloves, chopped finely

Oven temperature:
Gas Mark 3/160°C/325°F

A tremendous hit with those who like full but clear flavours, and good to look at too. A rich, smooth mixture of veal, almonds, cream and eggs is marbled with masses of chopped parsley, spiked with grated lime zest and chopped garlic. Called a 'gremolata' in Italy, the parsley combination is most often sprinkled on osso bucco, a stew of veal shin bones. I've used fresh lime zest in the recipe but lemon or orange would be just as good.

Preheat the oven. Process the veal with the eggs, cream, ground almonds and seasonings until as smooth as possible. Ideally, force the mixture through a fine sieve with the back of a soup ladle to ensure absolute smoothness.

Mix together the parsley, zest and garlic for the gremolata. Choose a shallow ovenproof dish, suitable for taking to the table, of about 600 ml (1 pint) capacity: I use a simple, blue-edged enamel pie dish. Into the dish spoon heaps of the meat mixture, sprinkling them generously with the gremolata to give a marbled effect. Press down firmly, cover with a lid or foil and bake in a bain-marie for 40–60 minutes, depending on the shape of the dish.

Serve in slices or squares cut from the dish at the table. The pâté should be chilled but not served directly from the refrigerator. Most people like just brown bread with this, but you could make it more important in a meal by serving it with a salad, perhaps sprinkled with oil and the juice from the lime you previously grated. You might also consider baking this in a conventionally shaped loaf tin and turning it out.

*Almond Veal Pâté Marbled with Fresh Lime Gremolata
Provençal Lamb and Spinach Pâté*

PROVENÇAL LAMB AND SPINACH PÂTÉ

Preparation time: 10 minutes
+ 45–60 minutes cooking + cooling

Makes 625 g (1¼ lb)

250 g (8 oz) frozen chopped spinach, thawed (175 g/ 6 oz drained weight)

500 g (1 lb) minced lamb

2 tablespoons dry white vermouth

1 tablespoon olive oil, plus extra for greasing

1 tablespoon finely chopped onion

2 garlic cloves, crushed or chopped finely

2 tablespoons chopped fresh parsley

½ teaspoon fresh thyme leaves or a pinch of dried thyme

2 tablespoons ground almonds

1 teaspoon ground cinnamon

1 teaspoon salt

½ teaspoon freshly ground black pepper

Oven temperature:
Gas Mark 5/190°C/375°F

Preheat the oven. Squeeze out as much water as possible from the spinach. Add the remaining ingredients and mix thoroughly. Press into a lightly oiled 500 g (1 lb) loaf tin, cover with foil and bake in a bain-marie for 45 minutes–1 hour.

Let the terrine cool completely in the tin. Pour off any excess juices and use them as a sauce for the pâté. Keep refrigerated, but allow the terrine to come to room temperature for about half an hour before serving.

GREEK LAMB AND BLACK OLIVE PÂTÉ

Preparation time: 10 minutes
+ 1 hour cooking + cooling

Makes about 750 g (1½ lb)

125 g (4 oz) vine leaves, blanched

75 g (3 oz) stoned black olives, preferably Kalamala olives, chopped roughly

2 tablespoons olive oil, plus extra for greasing

a few drops of wine vinegar

500 g (1 lb) minced lamb

250 g (8 oz) frozen chopped spinach , thawed (175 g/ 6 oz drained weight)

2 tablespoons white wine

1 tablespoon finely chopped onion

2 garlic cloves, crushed or chopped finely

2 tablespoons finely chopped fresh parsley

½ teaspoon dried oregano

2 teaspoons lemon juice

pepper, to taste

Oven temperature:
Gas Mark 5/190°C/375°F

Preheat the oven. Line a lightly oiled 500 g (1 lb) loaf tin with vine leaves, shiny–side outside, and sprinkle 25 g (1 oz) of the chopped olives over the base. Chop the remaining olives very finely (a food processor is easiest) with two teaspoons of the olive oil and the wine vinegar. Stir this olive paste with the remaining olive oil and the rest of the ingredients until very well blended. Add a little pepper if you like. Press into the lined tin, cover the top with more vine leaves and then a lid of foil. Bake in a bain–marie for 1 hour.

Let the pâté cool completely in the tin. Pour off any excess juices and use them as a sauce for the pâté. Keep refrigerated, but allow the pâté to come to room temperature for about half an hour before serving.

BRITISH RABBIT AND GAMMON BRAWN

Preparation time: 40 minutes
+ 2 hours cooking + chilling

Makes about 500 g (1 lb)

1 hock of gammon,
weighing about 750 g
(1½ lb)

500 g (1 lb) rabbit portions

150 ml (¼ pint) milk

6 black peppercorns

1 bay leaf

3 or 4 parsley stalks, crushed

600 ml (1 pint) water

leaves of a bunch of
watercress

11 g (¼ oz) envelope of
gelatine powder

Adapted from an idea mentioned in Dorothy Hartley's 'Food in Britain', this colourful combination of cubed pink gammon, pale rabbit and bright green watercress leaves in a white jelly looks terrific and has the comforting sort of flavour which people dub 'old-fashioned'. Highly recommended, although a somewhat time-consuming recipe.

In a large saucepan, cover the hock with cold water. Bring the water slowly to the boil and then drain it off. Add the rabbit portions, with the milk, peppercorns, bay leaf, parsley stalks and water. Bring to the boil, cover, and simmer very gently for about 2 hours until the meat falls from the bones. Remove the meat and reduce the cooking liquid by fast boiling until 450 ml (¾ pint) remains. Take all the meat from the bones.

In a suitable dish of about 750 ml (1¼-pint) capacity, make a layer of half the rabbit meat, followed by a quarter of the watercress leaves. Cut the gammon pieces to a similar size to those of the rabbit, add half the meat to the dish and then add another layer of watercress. Repeat the layers, ending with watercress.

Dissolve the gelatine in the hot reduced stock and pour it over. Leave for at least 24 hours and give it time to come almost to room temperature before cutting it, to enjoy the flavour at its best. I think you need only a little mustard and very good brown bread to enjoy this, but with a salad it would make a super lunch.

Greek Lamb and Black Olive Pâté
British Rabbit and Gammon Brawn

POULTRY

TEX-MEX TURKEY PÂTÉ WITH RED BEANS AND CHILI

Preparation time: 15 minutes + 50 minutes cooking + cooling

Makes 750 g (1½ lb)

500 g (1 lb) turkey breast fillets

50 g (2 oz) onion, chopped

1 garlic clove, crushed

432 g (15¼ oz) can of red kidney beans, rinsed and drained

1 tablespoon mild chili powder or seasoning

1 generous tablespoon tomato purée

6 tablespoons red wine

½ teaspoon salt

oil for greasing

Oven temperature:
Gas Mark 4/180°C/350°F

Wonderfully colourful to look at, this fascinating pâté proves how right the Mexicans and Texans were to combine their favourite foods to make modern Tex-Mex cuisine. Be sure to use chili powder and not pure chilli; the latter is merely cayenne pepper and adds nothing but heat to a mixture. Chili is a mixed spice, relying particularly on ground cumin to give flavour and excitement.

Preheat the oven. Chop 125 g (4 oz) of the turkey meat into neat dice and set aside. Put the remaining meat with the onion and garlic into a food processor and process until smooth. Set aside 50 g (2 oz) of the beans and add the remainder to the turkey paste, with the chili powder or seasoning, tomato purée, wine and salt. Process for another minute. Transfer to a bowl and stir through the reserved beans and turkey meat.

Grease a 1 kg (2 lb) loaf tin and spoon the mixture into it, making sure you fill all the corners and tapping the tin a few times to dispel any air pockets. Cover with a lid of greased foil, stand in a bain-marie and bake for about 50 minutes, until firm to touch. Allow to cool completely in the tin before umoulding or refrigerating. Once the loaf has been chilled, let it come to room temperature for 20–30 minutes before serving.

CHICKEN TONNATO IN A NEW MOULD

Preparation time: 30 minutes + chilling   Makes about 500 g (1 lb)

250 g (8 oz) boneless
chicken breast, skinned

100 ml (3 fl oz) white wine

200 g (7 oz) can of tuna in
brine, drained

300 ml (½ pint)
mayonnaise

½ teaspoon anchovy
essence, plus a little extra if
necessary

1 packet of powdered aspic

oil for greasing

25 g (1 oz) fresh parsley,
chopped coarsely

salt and freshly ground black
pepper

It is usual to use a thin, tuna-flavoured mayonnaise as a sauce for veal in Italy, but one of my most successful recipes on television used such a sauce for poached chicken. This repeats that combination very nicely to make a fascinating first course of subtle colour and full flavour. Naturally, you could substitute turkey, pork, veal or any other white meat.

Poach the chicken fillets in the wine with a little salt and pepper in a covered pan for about 12–15 minutes, until tender; take care not to overcook them or they will toughen. Leave them in the wine. When cool, remove the chicken fillets and cut them across at a slight angle into 1 cm (½-inch) slices. Reserve the wine.

Process the tuna with the mayonnaise and anchovy essence in a blender or food processor until smooth. Check the flavour and add a touch more anchovy essence if the fish flavour is not obvious; it should not be overpowering as it will develop somewhat.

Dissolve the aspic in the wine used to cook the chicken. Cool slightly and stir into the tuna mixture. Leave until it begins to thicken. Oil a 900 ml (1½-pint) decorative mould. Pour in a third of the tuna mixture, sprinkle with half the chopped parsley and top with half the sliced chicken, laid lengthways. Continue with a further layer of tuna mayonnaise, parsley and chicken, finishing with the remainder of the tuna. Cover and chill for several hours before turning out. Serve in slices, chilled but not directly from the refrigerator.

MEGHRIB CHICKEN PÂTÉ WITH SAFFRON PRAWNS

Preparation time: 15 minutes
+ 35–45 minutes cooking + cooling

Makes about 625 g (1¼ lb)

75 g (3 oz) softened butter

a pinch of powdered saffron

¼ teaspoon ground ginger

½ teaspoon paprika

75 g (3 oz) shelled prawns

250 g (8 oz) boneless chicken breast, skinned and chopped roughly

25 g (1 oz) ground almonds

2 whole eggs

1 egg white

150 ml (5 fl oz) carton of double cream

oil for greasing

salt and ground white pepper

Oven temperature:
Gas Mark 3/160°C/325°F

The Meghrib, north-western Africa, cooks some of the world's most voluptuous food, combining almonds and butter with such expensive spices as golden saffron. Morocco presents the best food by far, and this recipe is influenced by continuing Moroccan traditions.

Preheat the oven. Melt 15 g (½ oz) of the butter, add the saffron, ginger and paprika and then stir in the prawns. Set aside.

Put the chicken meat into a food processor and process until fairly smooth. Add the ground almonds, whole eggs and extra egg white and remaining butter and process again for a few seconds. Season well with salt and white pepper and then gradually add the cream, using the pulse action on the machine, until thoroughly blended.

Grease a 500 g (1 lb) loaf tin or mould. Carefully fold the prawns through the chicken mixture so they are evenly distributed, but do not over-mix: each prawn should sit in a trail of its buttery spices and bright saffron colour. Spoon the mixture into the tin, taking care to push the mixture into the corners and tapping the tin a few times to remove any air pockets. Level the top, cover with a sheet of oiled foil and put into a bain-marie. Cook for 35–45 minutes, until firm to touch. Allow to cool completely in the tin before turning out and refrigerating.

*Meghrib
Chicken Pâté
with Saffron Prawns*

*A Marble of
Light and Dark
Chicken Meats*

*Chicken and
Veal Pâté with Pimento Parcels*

65

CHICKEN AND VEAL PÂTÉ WITH PIMENTO PARCELS

Preparation time: 15 minutes
+ 30 minutes marinating + 50 minutes cooking

Makes about 500 g (1 lb)

375 g (12 oz) boneless chicken breast, skinned

2 tablespoons lemon juice

250 g (8 oz) minced veal

25 g (1 oz) onion, chopped

2 eggs

2 teaspoons finely grated lemon zest

2 tablespoons chopped fresh marjoram or 2 teaspoons dried marjoram

1 teaspoon salt

2 whole canned pimentos (red peppers)

oil for greasing

freshly ground black pepper

Oven temperature:
Gas Mark 3/160°C/325°F

With those who like visual delights as a first course, this will quickly become a favourite. A smooth, pale mousse of chicken and veal is sharpened with lemon and punctuated by tunnels of red pepper wrapped around strips of chicken breast.

Cut 125 g (4 oz) of the chicken into four neat pieces about 10 cm (4 inches) long. Sprinkle over the lemon juice and a generous amount of black pepper and leave to marinate for about 30 minutes. Preheat the oven.

Put the remaining chicken in a food processor, with the veal and onion, and process until fairly smooth. Add the eggs, zest, marjoram and salt and process again briefly.

Rinse the pimentos and pat them dry. Cut each in half and wrap one half around each piece of marinated chicken.

Grease a 1 kg (2 lb) loaf tin and spoon half the chicken and veal mixture into it. Level the surface and arrange the four wrapped fillets, in two lines, along the length of the tin. Cover with the remaining mixture. Level the top again and give the tin a couple of sharp taps to remove any air pockets. Cover with a sheet of greased foil, put into a bain-marie and bake for about 50 minutes. The mixture should feel firm to the touch. Allow the loaf to become quite cold in the tin before turning it out and refrigerating.

A MARBLE OF LIGHT AND DARK CHICKEN MEATS

Preparation time: 20 minutes
+ 45–50 minutes cooking + cooling

Makes about 750 g (1½ lb)

For the dark mixture:

300 g (10 oz) dark chicken meat (boneless thighs are ideal)

100 g (3½ oz) Bavarian soft cheese with horseradish

2 eggs

3 tablespoons double cream

1 teaspoon tomato purée

salt and freshly ground black pepper

For the light mixture:

300 g (10 oz) boneless chicken breasts, skinned

100 g (3½ oz) garlic-and-herb-flavoured soft cheese

2 eggs

3 tablespoons double cream

1 teaspoon finely grated lemon zest

oil for greasing

salt and freshly ground black pepper

Oven temperature:
Gas Mark 3/160°C/325°F

Really beautiful to look at, this is a stunning change from the usual layered effect of modern pâtés. Dark meat and light meat are flavoured separately and then swirled together in the same way that you make an old-fashioned marble cake. The cheeses used to give the contrasting flavours are bought ready-made in conveniently small quantities.

Preheat the oven. Make the dark mixture by processing the chicken with the cheese until it is fairly smooth. Add the eggs, cream and tomato purée and process again for a few seconds. Season lightly and set aside. Make the light meat mixture in the same way.

Grease a 1 kg (2 lb) loaf tin and put spoonfuls of the two mixtures randomly into it. Using the blade of a knife, lightly swirl the mixtures together, without blending them. Give the tin a couple of sharp taps to remove any air pockets and level the top, making sure the mixture reaches into the corners.

Cover with a sheet of greased foil, put into a bain-marie and bake for 45–50 minutes, until firm to touch. Allow the loaf to cool completely in the tin before turning it out or refrigerating.

DUCK WITH ORANGE PÂTÉ

Preparation time: 2 hours
+ 2½ hours cooking + cooling

Makes about 1.2 kg (2½ lb)

1.75 kg (4 lb) duck

2 tablespoons cognac

125 g (4 oz) rindless
sweetcure bacon

125 g (4 oz) onion, chopped

500 g (1 lb) minced pork

50 g (2 oz) dried white
breadcrumbs

2 large garlic cloves, chopped

2 teaspoons finely grated
orange rind

1 teaspoon dried thyme

½ teaspoon ground nutmeg

1 teaspoon salt

black pepper

butter (optional)

2 teaspoons finely grated
orange rind (optional)

For the stock:

oil (optional)

150 ml (¼ pint) orange juice

300 ml (½ pint) white wine

600 ml (1 pint) water

6 peppercorns

1 bay leaf

a few parsley stalks, crushed

2–3 slices of onion

1 stick of celery

Oven temperature:
Gas Mark 3/160°C/325°F

This makes a fairly big pâté, but as it uses a whole duck, this isn't surprising! Duck pâtés are notorious for shrinking, though, so be extra-careful not to turn the heat too high or cook for too long.

Remove all the skin from the duck and reserve it. Cut off the tail and preen gland, which is a small sac inside the parson's nose, and discard. Take off the breasts and cut them into strips. Put them in a shallow dish and pour over the cognac; leave to marinate for 20–30 minutes.

Reserve the bones and carcase, remove as much as possible of the remaining flesh from the duck and make it up with skin (cut up into small pieces) to weigh 750 g (1½ lb). Mince or process fairly finely with the bacon and onion; stir in the minced pork, breadcrumbs, garlic, orange rind, thyme, nutmeg and seasonings. Leave in a cool place to develop the flavour.

Chop the duck carcase and bones into smaller pieces. Make a strong duck stock by first browning the duck bones in hot oil or in a hot oven. Put the browned bones and other stock ingredients in a large saucepan. Simmer, covered, for 1 hour. Strain and reduce the stock by fast boiling until you have 250 ml (8 fl oz). Stir the stock into the prepared mixture.

Preheat the oven. Take an oval 1.75-litre (3-pint) dish, and fill it with the mixture; add the marinated strips of duck breast, either in a layer or in an irregular pattern. Stand the dish in a bain-marie and bake for 1¼–1½ hours, or until the juices are no longer running pink. Remove from the oven and leave to cool.

When the pâté is cold, the juices will have jellied and the fat set. There will be almost

*Orange-Cardamom Chicken Mousselines
with Orange Hollandaise
Duck with Orange Pâté*

enough fat to cover the pâté. Like this, it will keep uncut in a refrigerator for several weeks or more; it should certainly be kept for 48 hours before cutting, to allow the duck and the orange flavours to develop fully and mingle.

The fat has a lot of flavour, but if you don't want it, remove the whole pâté, clean it and present it in another, smaller bowl or on an oval platter, garnished simply. As a half-way measure, mix some of the fat with an equal quantity of melted butter, which will make it smoother. Stir in 2 teaspoons of finely grated orange rind and pour that back over the pâté. This tidies up the appearance and adds subtle flavours to the pâté.

Although something of a culinary cliché, the combination of a lightly chilled duck and orange pâté and a watercress salad is very hard to better.

ORANGE-CARDAMOM CHICKEN MOUSSELINES WITH ORANGE HOLLANDAISE

Preparation time: 25 minutes + 30 minutes chilling + 25 minutes cooking　　　Serves 6

For the mousselines:

375 g (12 oz) boneless chicken breasts, skinned and chopped roughly

1 tablespoon finely chopped shallot

125 g (4 oz) skimmed-milk soft cheese, or quark

1 egg

2 egg whites

the crushed seeds from 6 cardamom pods

2 teaspoons finely grated orange zest

4 tablespoons white wine

150 ml (5 fl oz) carton of double cream

To some purists, these mousselines served warm don't really qualify as pâtés at all. But I think they are the lightest and most elegant of all, especially this recipe of chicken breast perfumed with cardamom and served with a luscious orange hollandaise. They are not difficult to make, but life might be easier if there is someone to help when it comes to sauce-making and serving.

Preheat the oven. Put the roughly chopped chicken into a food processor with the shallot and process until fairly smooth. Add the soft cheese, egg and egg whites, cardamom seeds, orange zest, wine and salt and pepper. Process again for 30 seconds. Gradually add the double cream, using the pulsing action, until well blended. Transfer the mixture to a bowl, cover and refrigerate for 30 minutes.

Grease six small moulds and set them in a

oil for greasing

salt and ground white pepper

**For the orange
hollandaise:**

4 tablespoons orange juice

1 tablespoon white wine

½ teaspoon finely chopped
shallot

the seeds from 2 cardamom
pods

4 black peppercorns

1 small bay leaf

2 egg yolks

125 g (4 oz) butter, cubed

salt and pepper

To decorate:

julienne strips of orange
zest, peeled

salad leaves

Oven temperature:
Gas Mark 3/160°C/325°F

roasting tin. Divide the chilled mixture between the moulds, levelling the tops. Pour very hot water into the tin so that it is half-way up the moulds. Cover the tin with a dome of foil. Bake for 25 minutes, until a knife inserted in the middle comes out clean. Stand the mousselines in a warm place while you make the sauce, during which time most of any excess liquid will be reabsorbed.

To make the hollandaise sauce, put 2 table-spoons of the orange juice, with the wine, shallot, cardamom seeds, peppercorns, and bay leaf, in a small pan and boil until reduced to a couple of teaspoons. Put the egg yolks into a bowl and strain the reduced liquid over them. Stand the bowl over a saucepan of simmering water and whisk until the sauce has thickened. Add the butter, piece by piece, whisking all the time, until you have a smooth, thick sauce. Beat in the remaining orange juice and season the sauce with salt and pepper.

Unmould the mousselines on to warm plates. Put a spoonful of sauce on each plate and decorate with blanched julienne strips of orange peel and a little of something green.

MUSTARD CHICKEN PÂTÉ WITH HAM AND OLIVES

Preparation time: 20 minutes
+ 40–50 minutes cooking + cooling

Makes about 1 kg (2 lb)

---

375 g (12 oz) boneless
chicken breasts, skinned and
chopped roughly

25 g (1 oz) onion, chopped

175 g (6 oz) curd cheese

2 eggs

1½ tablespoons whole-
grain mustard

150 ml (5 fl oz) carton of
double cream

50 g (2 oz) stuffed green
olives, rinsed and dried

150 g (5 oz) cooked ham,
cut into small, neat chunks

oil for greasing

Oven temperature:
Gas Mark 3/160°C/325°F

---

*Bright with colour and lively with flavour, this is
perfect party fare: a light base of chicken patterned
with mustard seeds, chunks of ham and whole stuffed
olives.*

Preheat the oven. Put the roughly chopped
chicken mixture with the onion into a food
processor and process until fairly smooth. Add
the curd cheese, eggs and mustard and process
again for a few seconds. Gradually add the
cream, using the pulse action on the machine,
until thoroughly blended; do not over-mix. Stir
in the whole olives and the ham.

Grease a 1 kg (2 lb) loaf tin or terrine and turn
the mixture into it, giving a few sharp taps to
remove any air pockets and levelling the surface.
Cover with a sheet of oiled foil, or a lid, and put
into a bain-marie and bake for 40–50 minutes.
The pâté will feel firm to the touch. Allow to
cool in the tin completely before turning out or
refrigerating.

*Mustard Chicken Pâté with
Ham and Olives*

72

*Chicken Liver Pâté with
Butter and Cream*

*Turkey Pâté with
Apricots and Mint*

73

CHICKEN LIVER PÂTÉ WITH BUTTER AND CREAM

Preparation and cooking time: 20 minutes + cooling

Serves 4

50 g (2 oz) butter

50 g (2 oz) onion, chopped finely

1 garlic clove, chopped finely or crushed

250 g (8 oz) chicken livers

2 heaped tablespoons whipped double cream

2 tablespoons medium sherry or cognac

salt and freshly ground black pepper

To serve:

melted butter (optional)

The more common chicken liver pâtés are essentially spreads and rely on a high fat content to give them 'spreadability', as well as a pleasant texture. If you have no cream about the house, simply double the butter.

Melt the butter in a pan and gently cook the onion and garlic until really soft but not coloured. Add the chicken livers and cook over a medium heat for about 5 minutes or until cooked through but still with pink juices. Don't keep poking and turning them or they won't cook evenly and excess moisture won't be able to escape.

Let the mixture cool but not set, and then transfer to a liquidiser or a food processor and process until smooth. Fold in the whipped cream and sherry or cognac and season to taste. Spoon into one pretty container or four small ramekins and let cool with greaseproof paper or cling film pressed to the surface to prevent a skin forming. Serve like this or pour on some melted butter and decorate.

Note: Although you can process this when hot or warm if you are in a hurry, you do not get as light a result; whisking the fat content when it is set or almost so, incorporates more air.

VARIATION

- The addition of any number of fresh or dried herbs allows countless variations; ground thyme and rosemary are very good but so is fresh parsley. Green peppercorns, either processed with the mixture or roughly crushed and folded through, are particularly popular; if using them, you might also use vodka rather than sherry or cognac.

TURKEY PÂTÉ WITH APRICOTS AND MINT

Preparation time: 10 minutes
+ 1 hour cooking + cooling

Makes about 875 g (1¾ lb)

500 g (1 lb) dark turkey meat

250 g (8 oz) minced pork

125 g (4 oz) soft, ready-to-eat dried apricots, chopped roughly

150 ml (5 fl oz) dry white wine

1–2 teaspoons dried mint

½ tablespoon whole coriander seeds, lightly crushed

1 teaspoon salt

pepper

1–2 tablespoons cognac

Oven temperature:
Gas Mark 4/180°C/350°F

This is one of my favourite flavour combinations and the basis of a very popular Christmas recipe for stuffing turkey. Combining dried apricots and mint is a trick of the Middle East, and so I've also included a delightful eastern spice, coriander seed, whose orange-spicyness complements the other flavours perfectly. Although given as a pâté for slicing, this is also an excellent mixture for cooking in hot-water crust pastry as a superior raised pie.

Preheat the oven. Mince or process the turkey meat coarsely and mix well with the minced pork. Stir in the dried apricots, white wine, mint, coriander, salt, pepper and cognac. Pack into a 900 ml (1½-pint) loaf tin, cover with foil and put it into a bain-marie. Bake for about an hour or until the juice no longer runs pink. Allow to cool and then wrap and store the pâté for at least 24 hours before cutting.

A CONTEMPORARY GALANTINE OF DUCK, APPLES AND BLACK PUDDING

Preparation time: 1 hour
+ 2 hours cooking + cooling

Makes about 1.2 kg (3½ lb)

2 kg (4½ lb) duck

4 tablespoons Calvados

2 tablespoons semolina

375 g (12 oz) black pudding

liver from the duck

250 g (8 oz) Bramley apple, unpeeled, grated

2 eggs, separated

375 g (12 oz) celeriac, peeled and grated

1 tablespoon Dijon mustard

aspic powder for decoration (optional)

Galantines more properly belong to professional and restaurant kitchens, for few home cooks know the technique of boning, rolling and tying and fewer have containers big enough in which to poach them gently. But contemporary methods make them somewhat simpler, provided you have a small sharp knife, a roasting tin, cake rack, cling film and cooking foil.

Here, a boned duck is stuffed with grated apple and celeriac, plus black pudding, flavoured with Calvados. Startling as this combination might seem, it is very traditional in France. Clearly only for special occasions, this galatine handsomely repays the time you spend on it, in appearance, flavour and the number of compliments it will draw.

Boning the duck is the only process which takes time and care. Use a very sharp, sharply pointed knife. First cut down the back of the bird, and keeping the knife pointing always down towards the carcase, rather than up toward the skin, ease the skin and as much flesh as you can from the bone. When you get to the joints of the legs and wings, cut through the joints and then continue to cut the breast flesh away from the bone. Be exceptionally careful at the keel, the central bone of the breast, as the skin rests almost directly on that.

Once the central carcase is free of flesh, use the knife to scrape the flesh down the bones of the wings and legs. Cut off the final joint of the wing altogether; cut through the skin around the leg above the last joint. Remove all bones and turn the legs and wings in on themselves so that the flesh is inside. Cut off the tail and preen gland. Cut off half of the big flap of neck skin.

A Contemporary Galantine of Duck, Apples and Black Pudding

Spread out the duck, flesh side uppermost, and arrange so that the flesh is spread as evenly as possible on the skin. Sprinkle with one tablespoon of Calvados and then with the semolina. Skin the black pudding and mash it in a bowl with the duck's liver, 2 tablespoons of the grated apple, the egg yolks and remaining Calvados. Beat until well blended. Lightly whisk the egg whites. In a separate bowl, mix together the celeriac, lightly whisked egg whites and mustard, with the remaining grated apple.

Spread the celeriac mixture evenly over the duck, leaving a border around the edge. Form the black pudding mixture into a sausage shape and place it in the centre of the duck. Carefully fold the top, bottom, and sides of the duck over the filling, to make an evenly-shaped parcel. Now comes the contemporary part.

Normally, a galantine of this type would be tied with string and poached, but nowadays, even top French restaurants steam them wrapped in cling film. Take a length of wide film at least twice the length of the duck and roll the duck on to it, so the folded-over edges are underneath. Pull the cling film up the sides and then fold over the top and bottom. Repeat with another two layers of cling film.

Stand the prepared duck parcel on a rack over a roasting tin of hot water and cover it with a dome of foil sealed tightly around the edge of the tin. Steam for 2 hours at a moderate pace; if the water is steaming enough, the foil should be making a light tinkling sound. Too much or too little sound means too much or too little steam.

Let the galantine cool and then chill thoroughly in the cling film. Remove the film and clean up the galantine, pressing kitchen paper firmly on the surface all over and letting it absorb all the fat from the pores.

You can serve this as it is, thinly sliced, but for the sake of presentation it would be more usual to make up a packet of aspic jelly according to the instructions, and, when it is cold but not setting, to paint this on the galantine.

VARIATION

- Make up the aspic with only half the recommended amount of liquid and when it is cold, stir it into a mixture of equal quantities of good mayonnaise, and whipped cream. The usual proportions are 300 ml (½ pint) aspic jelly to 300 ml (½ pint) mixed mayonnaise and cream. This mixture is known as a chaudfroid, and prettily cut pieces of vegetables and fruit can be pressed into the surface before it sets.

A LIGHT CARIBBEAN MOUSSE OF CHICKEN, MANGO AND GINGER

Preparation time: 10 minutes + 30 minutes chilling + 40 minutes cooking + cooling   Serves 4–6

250 g (8 oz) boneless chicken breast, skinned and chopped roughly

1 ripe mango

2 egg whites

1 whole egg

2 tablespoons white rum, plus a little extra

1 teaspoon peeled grated root ginger

100 ml (3 fl oz) double cream

oil for greasing

a little grated lime peel

salt and pepper

Oven temperature:
Gas Mark 3/160°C/325°F

Baked in a loaf tin but as light as a mousse, chicken is here flavoured with all your favourite Caribbean tastes: fresh mango, fresh ginger and white rum.

Preheat the oven. Put the chopped chicken into a food processor and process until fairly smooth. Cut the mango in two lengthways and set one half aside. Peel and roughly chop the other half and add it to the chicken, with the egg whites and egg, rum and ginger. Process until smooth. Season generously and then gradually add the double cream, taking care not to over-process. Transfer the mixture to a bowl, cover and chill for 30 minutes.

Grease a 500 g (1 lb) loaf tin, or 4–6 small moulds. Spoon the mixture into the prepared containers, level the top(s), cover each with foil and stand them in a bain-marie. Bake the larger tin for about 40 minutes; individual ones will take about 25 minutes. Serve the mousseline warm, garnished with the reserved mango, sliced or chopped and lightly bathed in white rum into which you have grated a little fresh lime peel. This is equally marvellous for having been left to its own devices for several days so that the flavours develop. Slightly chill before serving.

SOME THOUGHTS ON SERVING CHICKEN LIVER PÂTÉS

The most common way to serve chicken liver pâtés, which are essentially spreads, is with bread rolls or with toast, and very nice too for a few people or a family meal. But rolls can look as if you've not made an effort on special occasions, and toast takes too much trouble to eat if you guests won't be sitting. There is a better and more contemporary solution.

These days, I scoop chicken liver pâté into even shapes using a warm spoon or small ice cream scoop. I place the scoops on a small amount of mixed salad leaves, which have been torn into mangeable-size pieces, on a flat plate. Then I dress both pâté and salad with a simple dressing, not too sharp, that gives the pâté a glistening coat. This looks marvellous and has the distinct advantage that you can eat it with just a fork or with a knife and fork: much easier at 'stand-up' buffets. Good, warmed bread rolls would be a sensible touch, but toast is totally unnecessary.

The dressing should be made from either a nut oil or a bland oil like grapeseed, rather than olive oil, and lemon or lime juice instead of vinegar. More interestingly, I often flavour a scant tablespoon of vodka per person with a little fresh lime juice and spoon that first on to the pâté scoops and then over the salad. For final bite, I finally grate fresh lime peel – just a little – over each plate.

CHOPPED LIVER

This is probably the best-known chicken liver dish in the world, and a traditional Jewish speciality. Considering how widespread Jewish communities have been, it is hardly surprising that there are hundreds, if not thousands, of variations. In Britain, and often in America, chopped liver includes raw onion: yet the first time I was in Israel only cooked onion seemed popular, and this certainly gives a milder, more acceptable pâté, for you should never serve anything including raw onion at a dinner party or at any meal where good wines or puddings are also offered. Suit yourself; here are two variations.

Israeli chopped liver

Preparation and cooking time: 20 minutes   Makes about 750 g (1½ lb)

oil or chicken fat for frying

250 g (8 oz) onions, sliced

500 g (1 lb) chicken livers

6 hard-boiled eggs, shelled

melted butter (optional)

salt and pepper, to taste

Heat the oil and fry the onions until very soft and golden brown, about 10 minutes: if you have some chicken fat, use this instead of oil. Remove the onions and drain them on kitchen paper. Trim the chicken livers, cutting off any patches of green. Add a little more oil or fat to the pan, if necessary, and fry the livers until they are just cooked through. Don't let them shrink, shrivel or dry.

With the fine blade of a mincer or a food processor, reduce the onions, chicken livers and 5 of the eggs to a paste: the exact texture can be varied according to your preference. Season with salt and pepper, and whisk in some extra oil or chicken fat for a nice consistency. If you are not Jewish, you can use melted butter, of course. Turn into a bowl.

Chop separately the white and the yolk of the remaining egg and sprinkle them on willy-nilly, or in some pleasing pattern.

British chopped liver

Preparation and cooking time: 10 minutes   Makes about 500 g (1 lb)

For 500 g (1 lb) trimmed chicken livers cooked in oil, chicken fat or butter, you also need a small onion, 2 or 3 hard-boiled eggs and 2 tablespoons of fresh white breadcrumbs. Make as above, season and sprinkle with the remaining egg, chopped.

Note: Both versions are equally good, but more expensive, made with calves' liver. I can't imagine any serious cook or eater combining raw onion with calves' liver.

CHICKEN LIVER PÂTÉ WITH BUTTERED APPLE AND CALVADOS

Preparation and cooking time:
20 minutes + chilling

Makes about 625 g (1¼ lb)

1 small Golden Delicious apple

75 g (3 oz) unsalted butter, plus a little extra if wished

3 tablespoons of Calvados, plus a little extra if wished

125 g (4 oz) streaky bacon, chopped

50 g (2 oz) onion, chopped

375 g (12 oz) chicken livers, trimmed

freshly ground black pepper

To decorate:

chopped, toasted hazelnuts (optional)

A truly delicious reminder of holidays in Normandy. Cubes of apples cooked in butter, folded into a light chicken liver pâté flavoured with Calvados. Although planned to be eaten cold, it is famously good warm.

Cut the apple into quarters, core and peel it and then cut the quarters lengthways and across to give even segments. Melt 50 g (2 oz) of the butter in a small pan and add the prepared apple plus 1 tablespoon of the Calvados and cook gently until most of the butter has been absorbed.

Melt the remaining butter and cook the bacon and onion until the fat has rendered and the onion is soft. Add the livers and cook until lightly browned but still slightly pink in the centre.

Remove the apples carefully from their pan and reserve. Swirl out the pan with the remaining Calvados. Pour this into a food processor or blender, adding the cooked bacon, onion and livers and work to a purée.

Spoon out of the machine and carefully fold the apple pieces through the pâté; season with a little pepper and transfer to a pretty dish. Allow to cool with greaseproof paper or cling film pressed to the surface. Serve as it is or cover with melted butter lightly flavoured with Calvados. A sprinkling of chopped, toasted hazelnuts would be a nice addition.

VEGETABLES

MUSHROOM AND BULGAR PÂTÉ

Preparation time: 15 minutes   Makes about 500 g (1 lb)
+ 40 minutes baking if necessary

1½ tablespoons olive oil, plus extra for greasing

50 g (2 oz) coarse bulgar

50 g (2 oz) butter

250 g (8 oz) mushrooms, chopped finely

1 tablespoon finely chopped onion

½ garlic clove, chopped finely

2 generous tablespoons chopped parsley

¼ teaspoon dried thyme

1 tablespoon lemon or lime juice

200 g (7 oz) fromage frais

2 eggs

salt and pepper

Oven temperature:
Gas Mark 4/180°C/350°F

This is really two pâtés in one; you can make either a simple version that is not baked in the oven, or add cheese and eggs to make a lighter, more elegant loaf that must be baked. Both retain a rich mushroom flavour and the rewarding texture of bulgar: this is sometimes known incorrectly as cracked wheat but is in fact boiled wheat that has been dried to a paste and then ground, whereas cracked wheat is uncooked.

Preheat the oven. Heat 1 tablespoon of the oil in a small pan and fry the bulgar over a high heat until browned.

Heat the remaining oil with the butter in a wide pan and fry the mushrooms, onion and garlic for 5 minutes over a fairly high heat, to bubble off most of the liquid. Stir in the herbs, and lemon or lime juice, and season well.

Add the bulgar to the mixture. At this stage, you can simply turn the mixture into a bowl and let it set. Otherwise, continue by combining it with the fromage frais and eggs and beat very well. Turn into a greased 500 g (1 lb) loaf tin, seal tightly with a lid of foil and place in a bain-marie. Bake for 40 minutes or until slightly risen and firm to the touch.

CARROT LOAF WITH APRICOTS AND ORANGE

Preparation time: 50 minutes
+ 50 minutes cooking + cooling

Makes about 625 g (1¼ lb)

250 g (8 oz) carrots, peeled and sliced thinly

150 ml (¼ pint) orange juice

83 g (3 oz) packet stuffing mix with apricots and sultanas

250 g (8 oz) skimmed milk soft cheese or curd cheese

3 eggs, beaten

freshly ground black pepper

oil for greasing

Oven temperature:
Gas Mark 4/180°C/350°F

Another fast-to-make pâté; you can make this with any stuffing mix that contains nuts or dried fruit, and add a few chopped dried apricots. The combination of carrots with apricots and orange is well known in the eastern Mediterranean and looks and tastes especially festive.

Cook the carrots gently in the orange juice in a covered pan until they are very tender; this might take 45 minutes. Preheat the oven. Transfer the carrots to a food processor or blender and purée them. Remove from the processor and gradually add the stuffing mix, cheese, eggs and seasoning, beating everything together in a large bowl until thoroughly mixed.
Line the base of a 500 g (1 lb) loaf tin with greaseproof paper. Spoon the mixture into it, pressing it into the corners and levelling the top. Seal with a sheet of oiled foil, stand the tin in a bain-marie and bake in the preheated oven for about 50 minutes, or until firm to touch. Allow to cool in the tin before turning it out.

POTTED PEAS

Preparation time: 10 minutes + chilling

Makes about 500 g (1 lb)

375 g (12 oz) frozen peas

62.5 g (2.2 oz) packet of soft cream cheese

62.5 g (2.2. oz) packet of butter with black pepper

This is a particularly useful idea when you must make a variety of pâtés for a buffet table, as it introduces a variety of contrasting colours and textures that complement meat and fish dishes.

Cover the peas with cold water, bring the water to the boil and drain immediately. Put the peas into a food processor or blender with the remaining ingredients and process thoroughly. Pack into the pots and chill thoroughly.

Carrot Loaf with Apricots and Orange
Potted Peas

A PATTERNED VEGETABLE PÂTÉ

Preparation time: 45 minutes
+ 1¼ hours cooking

Makes about 2 kg (4 lb)

1 kg (2 lb) root vegetables, scrubbed

450 ml (¾ pint) milk or single cream

50 g (2 oz) butter

225 g (8 oz) carton of semi-skimmed milk soft cheese

8 eggs

4 tablespoons lemon juice

1 kg (2 lb) vegetables, cut in thin strips

oil for greasing

a packet of vine leaves, blanched

salt and white pepper

Oven temperature:
Gas Mark 4/180°C/350°F

There has been a great vogue for pâtés containing layers of contrasting vegetables. But these were not usually vegetarian as the vegetables were cooked in a mousse of ham or chicken, and were often overpowered in flavour. A waste of time and money. Here the base is well flavoured root vegetables and the flavours of the other vegetables are carefully highlighted. Thus, in spite of the long cooking needed, you are rewarded with almost as much flavour as you started with.

It is possible to make half the quantity in a 500 g (1 lb) loaf tin, but the fiddle is increased rather than decreased so I always make a bigger one.

Your first task is to determine the eventual flavour and appearance of the pâté by the choice of vegetables. I like to use just parsnip for the base, which gives a fabulous pale colour and elegant flavour: but so does carrot or a mixture of carrot and parsnip. Celeriac gives a creamy pâté with a distinct but light celery flavour that is unexpected and refreshing; this vegetable needs to be peeled, not merely scrubbed.

Cut up the root vegetables roughly and poach them until they are tender in the milk or cream, with the butter. Liquidise and sieve the purée and let it cool to room temperature. Beat in the cheese, eggs and lemon juice and then season lightly with salt and white pepper. Do not attempt to do this when the vegetable purée is hot or warm or the texture of the cheese will be lost.

Preheat the oven. Now comes the creative part. The vegetables you are layering in the mixture should not be pre-cooked but must each be flavoured with something that will heighten its own flavour. Choose from one of the ideas under 'variations', below, or make up your own version.

Whatever you decide, first lightly oil a large loaf tin of 1.75-litre (3-pint) capacity and line it with vine leaves which have been soaked in hot water for a while and drained. Arrange them shiny-side outside and use bigger ones on the side, so there will be some to overlap. Arrange your vegetables in order of weight and after ladling in a first, thin layer of the vegetable purée, arrange the heaviest vegetable on that. Continue ladling in the purée and arranging the prepared vegetables, making the lines lengthways rather than across or you'll not make an even pattern. When everything is used up, add a layer of vine leaves and interleave it with those sticking up the side. Cover the tin with a dome of foil tightly sealed to the top edge and stand it in a bain-marie. Bake for 1¼ hours or until the top of the middle of the pâté is firm to touch.

Let cool completely and then refrigerate before turning out. Serve only lightly chilled, perhaps with a flavoured soured cream or a very reduced tomato sauce – or both.

VARIATIONS

- You could use just one vegetable, say carrots, and flavour each layer differently – with thyme, mint, orange zest, cumin seeds and so on.
- Use 3 or 4 vegetables but flavour with the same herb or spice – haricot beans (the frozen ones are terrific), carrots, canned artichoke bottoms and peas all go very nicely with dill weed.
- Or flavour each layer separately – carrot or turnip with masses of parsley and a little lemon or orange zest, celeriac with garlic and horseradish, fennel with olive oil and mustard.
- Or make a layer just of herbs, ideally, parsley chopped with others that are fresh.
- Or make a layer of a herb-flavoured cheese, of your own making or bought ready-made.
- If you are not a vegetarian you might consider some rows or layers of chicken breast, cubes of ham or strips of tongue. But flavour these, too, with alcohol, grated orange zest, fresh herbs and the like.

RED LENTILS AND CUMIN PÂTÉ

Preparation time: 5 minutes
+ 1½–1¾ hours cooking

Makes about 250 g (½ lb)

250 g (8 oz) red lentils

water

125 g (4 oz) skimmed milk soft cheese

2 teaspoons wine vinegar

1 teaspoon salt

2 teaspoons ground cumin

4 eggs, beaten

oil for greasing

Oven temperature:
Gas Mark 4/180°C/350°F

The smoky flavour of red lentils has long been a vegetarians' favourite way to make pâtés. Combined with lemony-peppery cumin, their rather homely flavour increases in sophistication and appeal.

Cook the lentils to a pulp in just enough water to cover them, about 40–50 minutes. Preheat the oven. In a large bowl, gradually beat the remaining ingredients into the cooked lentils. Line the base of a 500 g (1 lb) loaf tin. Spoon in the mixture, pressing it into the corners. Cover with a sheet of oiled foil, stand the tin in a bain-marie and bake it for 50–55 minutes, until firm to touch. Allow to cool in the tin before turning out.

Red Lentils and Cumin Pâté

A Patterned Vegetable Pâté

*Leek and Hazelnut
Party Terrine*

89

LEEK AND HAZELNUT PARTY TERRINE

Preparation time: 30 minutes
+ 1–1¼ hours cooking

Makes about 1.2 kg (2¼ lb)

750 g (1½ lb) trimmed
leeks, sliced finely

75 g (3 oz) butter

4 tablespoons white wine

85 g (3 oz) packet stuffing
mix with hazelnuts and
herbs

175 g (6 oz) semi-skimmed
soft cheese or curd cheese

4 eggs, beaten

50 g (2 oz) chopped toasted
hazelnuts

oil for greasing

1 packet of vine leaves,
blanched

Oven temperature:
Gas Mark 4/180°C/350°F

*Beautifully coloured and flavoured, dotted with
chopped hazelnuts, and wrapped in shining green
vine leaves, this sophisticated pâté can also be made
with any nut or herb stuffing mix, except a sage and
onion one.*

Preheat the oven. Cook the leeks with the butter
in a covered pan over a low heat until they are
tender but still bright green. Put them into a
food processor or blender with the wine and
purée them. Transfer to a large bowl and stir in
the stuffing mix, the cheese and the eggs. When
thoroughly blended, add the nuts.

Line an oiled 1 kg (2 lb) terrine or loaf tin with
the vine leaves, shiny-side out, allowing an
overlap on top. Fill with the leek mixture, taking
care to press it into the corners. Level the top,
wrap over the leaves from the sides and cover
with additional leaves if necessary. Oil a large
sheet of foil and seal the terrine securely. Stand
the tin in a bain-marie and bake for 1–1¼ hours,
depending on its depth. The top should feel firm
to touch. Allow the terrine to cool completely in
the tin before turning it out or refrigerating it.

BLUE CHEESE WITH WALNUTS PÂTÉ

Preparation time: 10 minutes

Makes about 15

100 g (3½ oz) Jutland
Blue full-fat cheese

50 g (2 oz) butter

50 g (2 oz) Cheese Thins
(cheese biscuits), crushed

75 g (3 oz) chopped
walnuts, toasted

Put the cheese and butter in a bowl and melt
them gently over a pan of simmering water or in
a microwave oven on medium power. Stir in the
biscuits and a good third of the walnuts. Cover
and chill for about an hour, until firm enough to
handle.

Crush the remaining walnuts and put them on
a small plate. Form the cheese mixture into
walnut-size balls and roll them in the crushed
nuts. Chill again for at least 30 minutes. Serve as
appetisers, or as a starter.

ENGLISH PEASE PUDDING WITH CRISPY ONION AND BACON

Preparation and cooking time: 30 minutes + 55–60 minutes cooking + cooling

Makes about 500 g (1 lb)

100 g (3½ oz) smoked streaky bacon, chopped

125 g (4 oz) onion, chopped

1 tablespoon oil (optional), plus extra for greasing

439 g (15½ oz) can of pease pudding

3 eggs, beaten

freshly ground black pepper

Oven temperature:
Gas Mark 4/180°C/350°F

The pease pudding available in cans is every bit as good as home-made, but cheaper and time-saving. Its rugged flavour is combined here with two other traditional favourites, crisp onion and bacon, in this pâté. A special favourite with men, it would be a perfect choice for the spread after winter football matches.

Preheat the oven. Cook the bacon until some of the fat is released; add the onion and continue cooking over moderate heat until both are very brown and crisp, adding the oil if necessary to prevent sticking. Be patient as it takes some time to do this properly without burning.

Beat together the pease pudding, eggs and plenty of pepper. Stir in the bacon and onion, with all the fat from the pan.

Line the base of a 500 g (1 lb) loaf tin with greaseproof paper. Spoon the mixture into it, pressing it into the corners. Level the top, cover with a piece of oiled foil and stand the tin in a bain-marie; bake for about 55–60 minutes, until firm to touch. Allow to cool in the tin before turning out.

GORGONZOLA AND PINE KERNELS PÂTÉ

Preparation time: 15 minutes

Serves 6

250 g (8 oz) Gorgonzola cheese, crumbled

2 hard-boiled eggs

50 g (2 oz) butter, softened

2 tablespoons pine kernels, lightly toasted

melted butter, optional

Blend the cheese with the egg yolks and butter. Chop the egg whites finely and stir them into the mixture, with the pine kernels. Pack into six small ramekins or suitable pots and chill thoroughly.

This potted cheese will keep for 2–3 days in the refrigerator; if you need to keep it a little longer (up to 10 days) cover with a thin layer of melted butter.

WENSLEYDALE WITH APPLE PÂTÉ

Preparation time: 10 minutes   Makes about 250 g (½ lb)

50 g (2 oz) unsalted butter

1 medium-size eating apple, peeled, cored and neatly diced

125 g (4 oz) Wensleydale cheese, grated or crumbled finely

62.5 (2.2 oz) packet creamery full-fat cheese

40 g (1½ oz) walnuts, crushed

Melt the butter in a small pan, add the apple and cook very gently until soft, about 10 minutes. Beat together the two cheeses and carefully fold through the cooked apples and butter. Chill the mixture for about an hour, until firm enough to handle.

Form into two barrels, each about 11 × 2.5 cm (4½ × 1 inches). Roll in the crushed nuts and chill again for several hours. Slice the rolls fairly thinly; it's nice on small plates with a salad of decorative leaves, tossed in walnut oil dressing, with a little extra walnut oil drizzled over the cheese slices.

WELSH CHEESE AND LEEKS

Preparation and cooking time: 20 minutes + chilling   Serves 2

2 fat leeks, about 3½ cm (1½ inches) in diameter

125 g (4 oz) Caerphilly cheese, crumbled

50 g (2 oz) butter, softened

2 teaspoons smooth Dijon mustard

To serve:

salad leaves

vinaigrette dressing

Wash the leeks thoroughly and trim them to 10 cm (4 inches) long. Cook in boiling salted water for 10 minutes. Drain and cool under running water. Carefully remove two outer 'skins' from each leek, without cutting or tearing them, and dry on kitchen paper.

Chop the remaining cooked leek finely and beat it together with the other ingredients, until well blended. Using a teaspoon and working from both ends, fill the leek 'skins' with the cheese mixture. Cover and chill until firm.

Cut each leek into five slices and arrange them on a plate with pretty salad leaves. Drizzle with well flavoured vinaigrette dressing.

Gorgonzola and Pine Kernels
Wensleydale with Apple Pâté
Welsh Cheese and Leeks

CELEBRATION CHEESE PÂTÉ

Preparation time: 10 minutes   Makes 500 g (1 lb)

175 g (6 oz) skimmed-milk soft cheese

50 g (2 oz) butter, softened

250 g (8 oz) mature Cheddar cheese, grated

Make cheese a star attraction on a buffet table, rather than a uninspired alternative. It will be appreciated by many guests, especially if you concoct exciting variations, but avoid using red wine: it will discolour the pâté, as well as tasting unpleasant.

Beat together the soft cheese and butter. When it is soft, gradually mix in the grated Cheddar and beat until thoroughly blended. Then follow one of the ideas for flavourings under 'Variations', below.

Chill the mixture for an hour or so; then turn it on to a clean surface and shape it into a roll about 4 cm (1½ inches) in diameter. Roll it in finely chopped parsley or dill, in sweet paprika, parmesan cheese, crushed nuts or cracker crumbs. Wrap in cling film or foil and refrigerate for several hours, until very firm. Serve the roll very thinly sliced, with biscuits or salad.

If you prefer, chill the pâté and use a melon-baller to make bite-sized balls; toss them in a coating, or don't, as you please.

VARIATIONS

- 2–3 tablespoons fresh herbs, chopped, plus 1–2 teaspoons finely grated lemon zest.
- 50 g (2 oz) walnuts, toasted or not, and chopped fairly finely, plus 1–2 teaspoons finely grated orange rind and a little cognac, to taste.
- 1–2 teaspoons grated onion *or* finely chopped spring onion, plus ¼ teaspoon freshly grated nutmeg.
- 50 g (2 oz) cashew or peanuts, chopped, plus 1–2 teaspoons Dijon mustard.
- For a richer pâté, replace the skimmed-milk cheese with curd cheese or cream cheese; for instant flavouring, use soft cream cheese with garlic and herbs, or soft cream cheese with horseradish.

INDEX TO RECIPES

Design and layout: Ken Vail Graphic Design
Illustrations: Mandy Doyle
Photography: Laurie Evans
Stylist: Lesley Richardson
Food preparation for photography: Allyson Birch
Typesetting: Westholme Graphics
Printed and bound by Balding & Mansell Ltd,
Wisbech, Cambs